ZODIAC

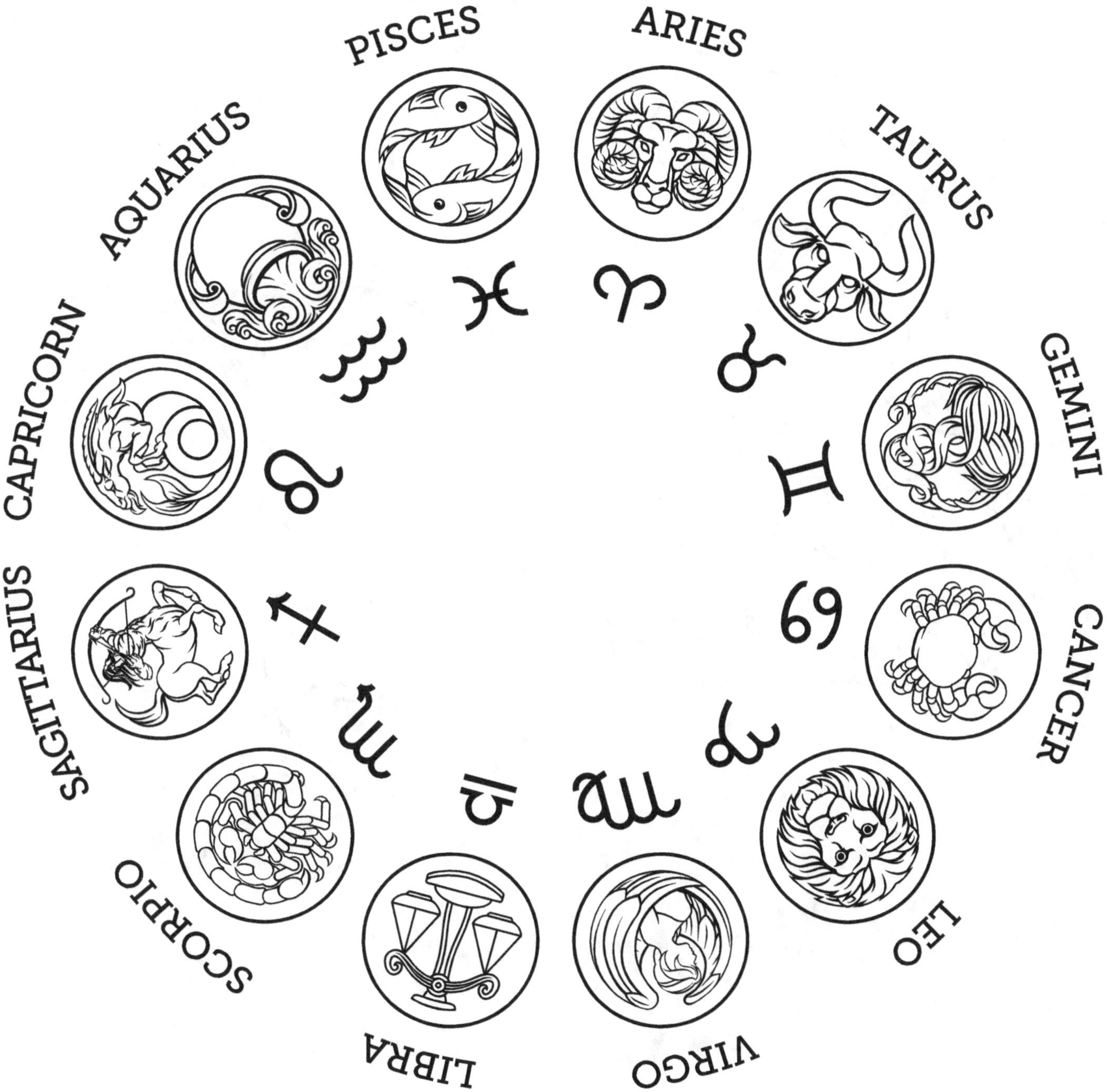

CAPRICORN

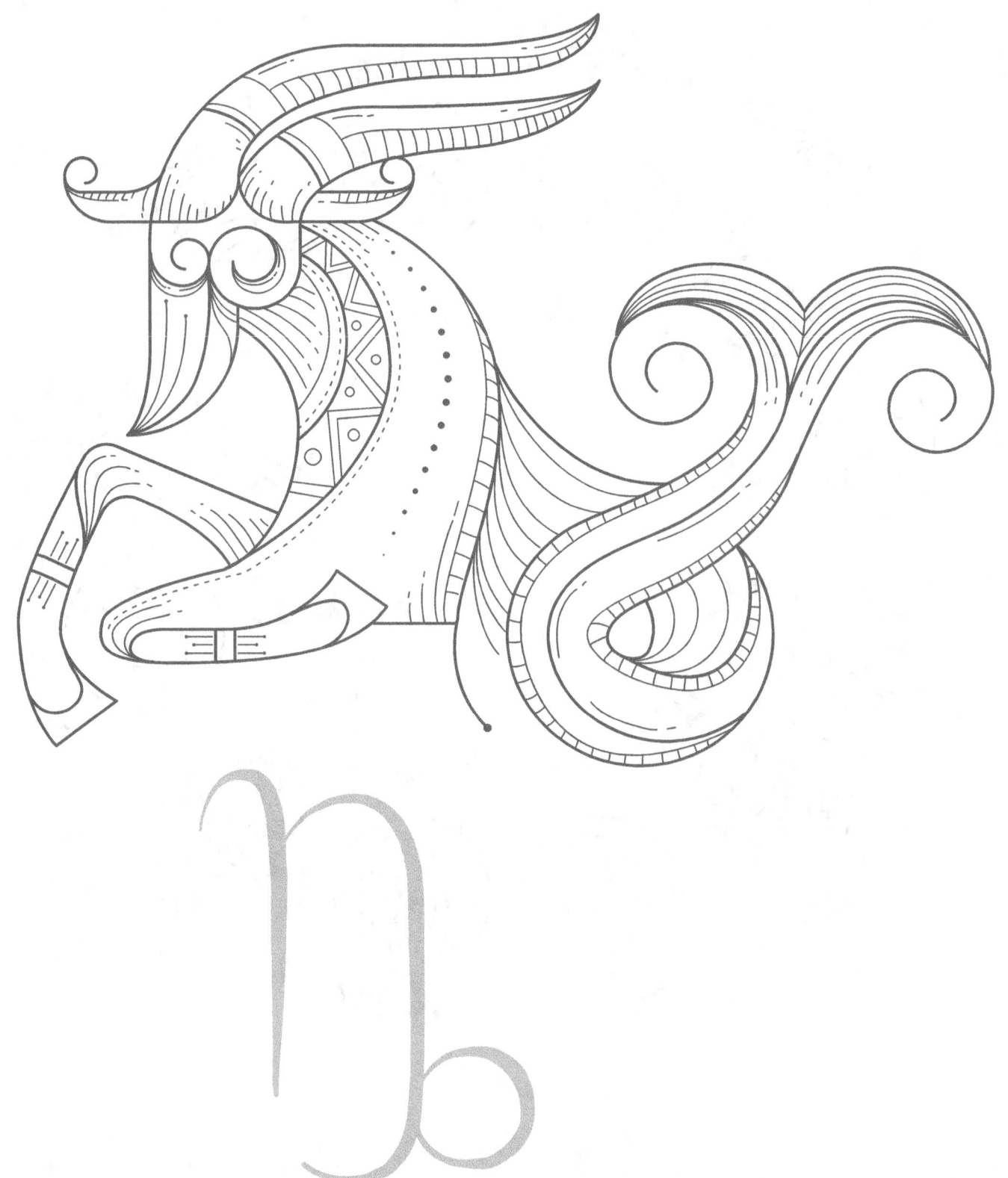

AQUARIUS

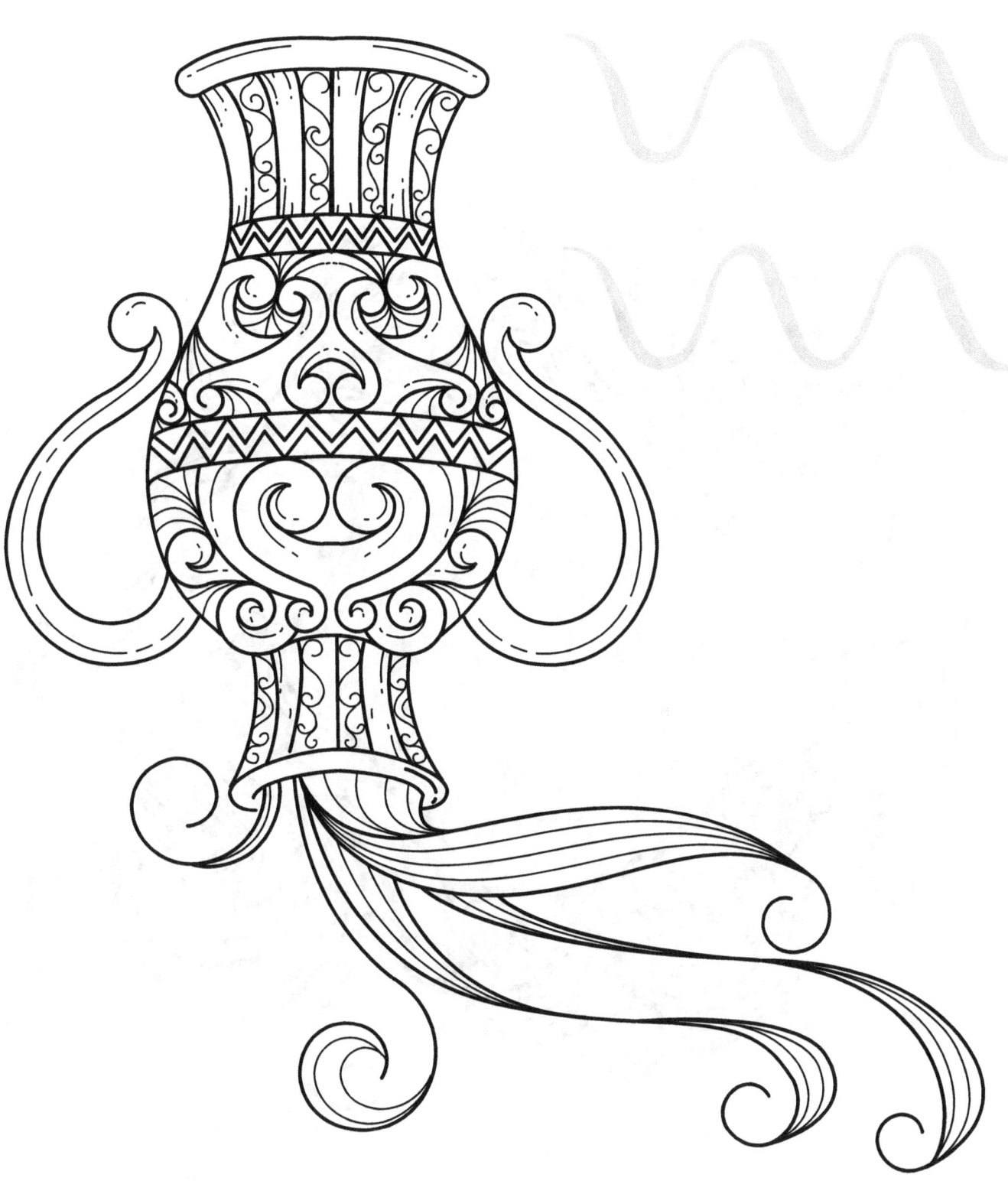

PISCES

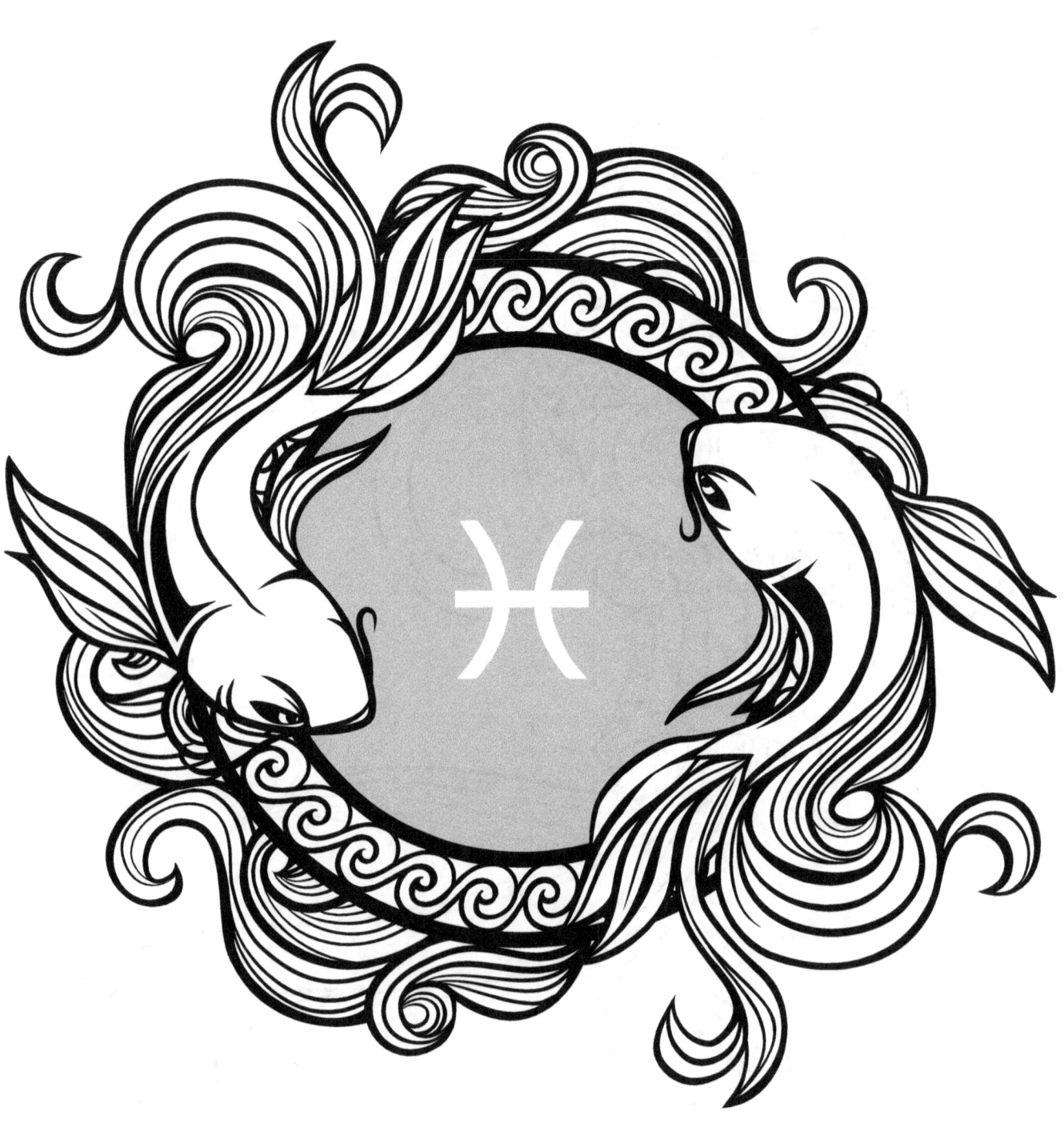

ARIES

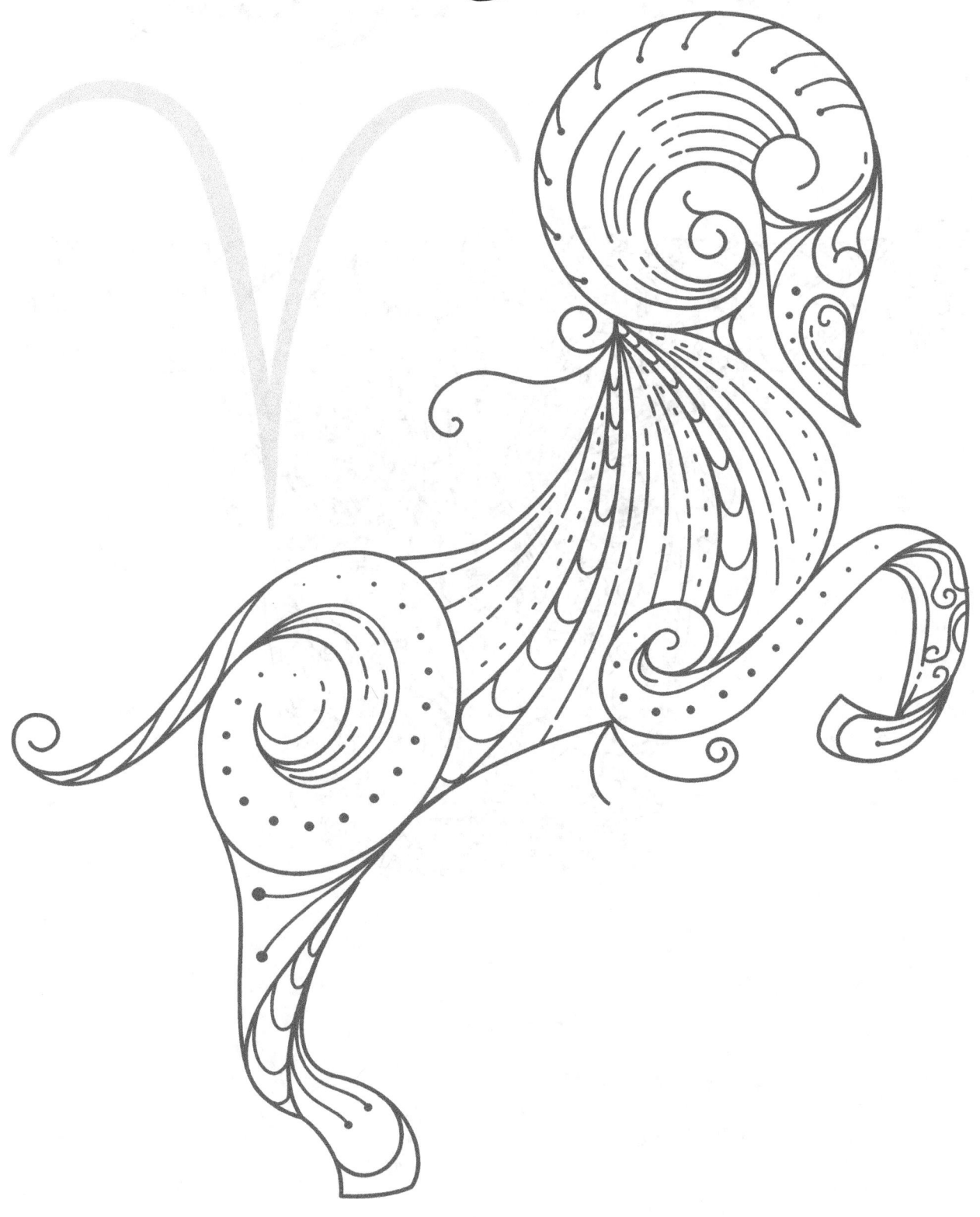

TAURUS

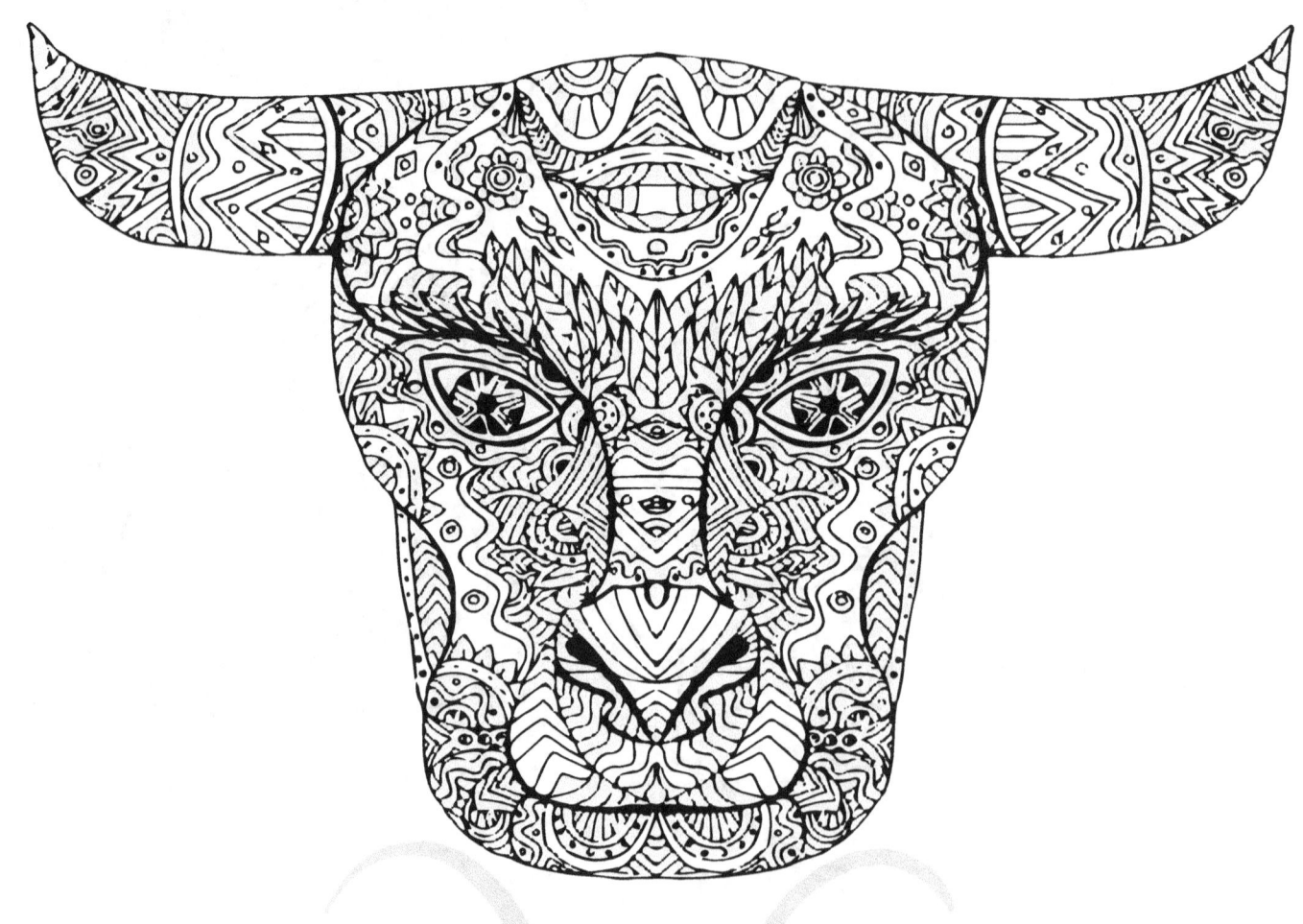

GEMINI

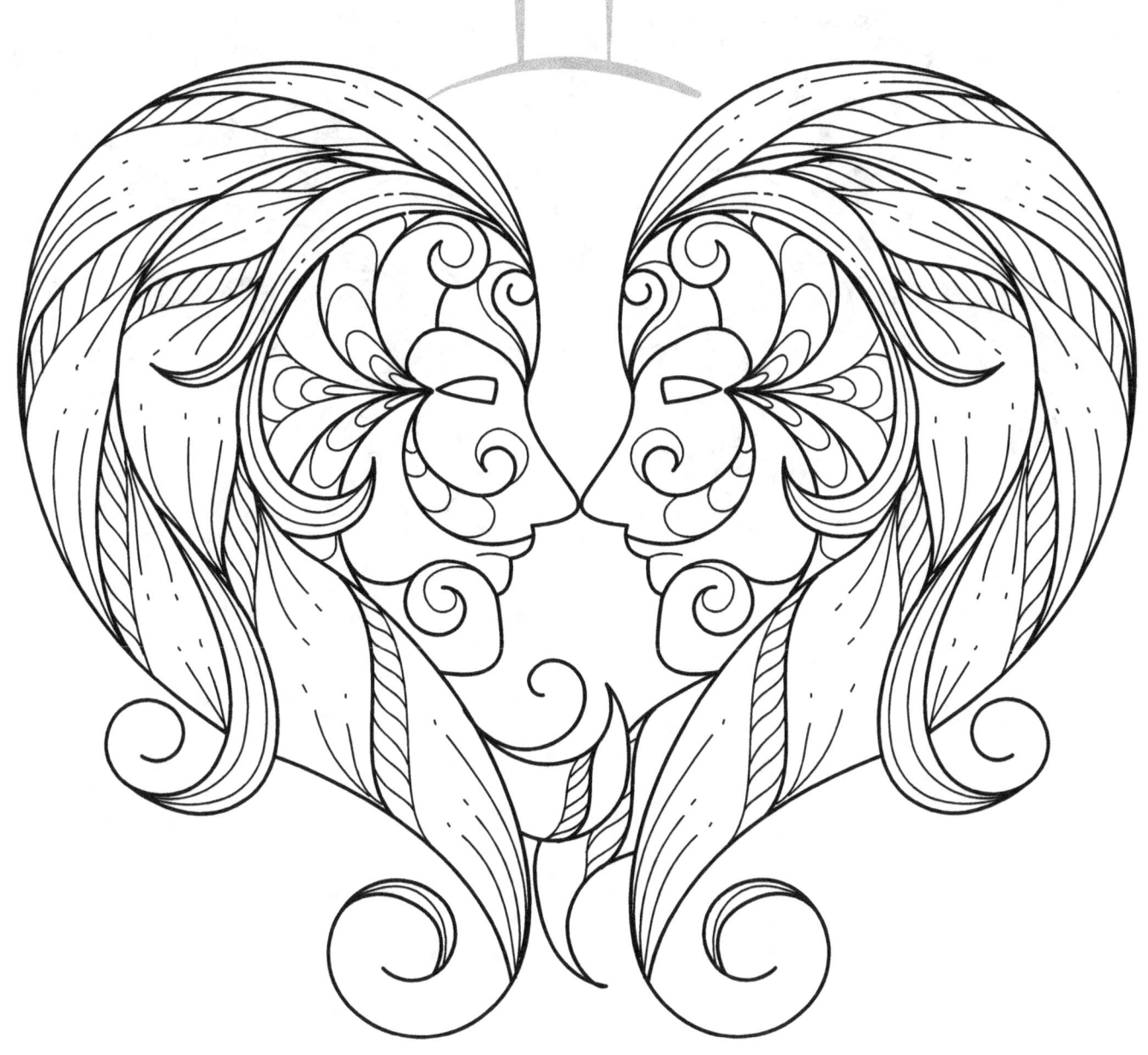

CANCER

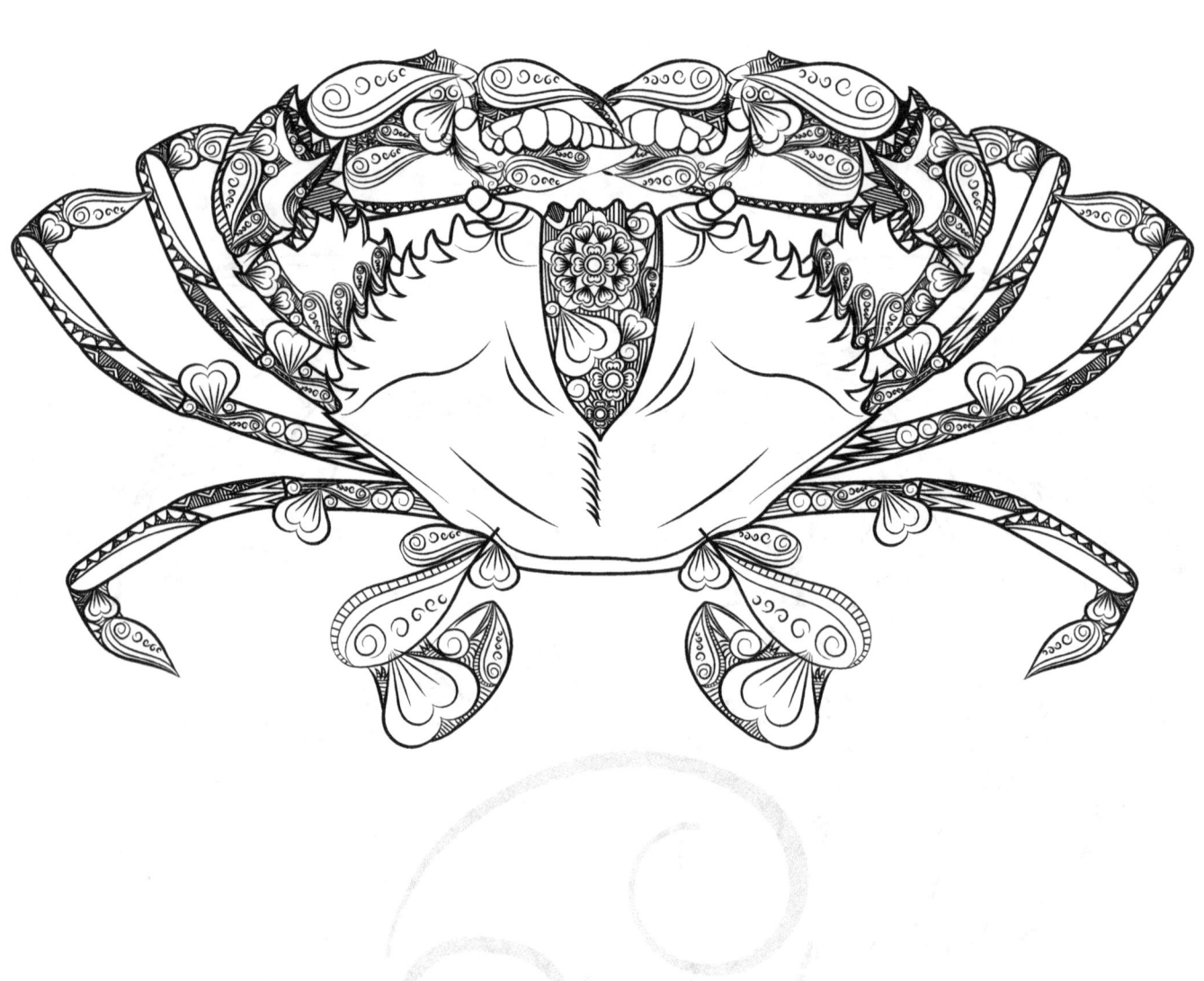

LEO

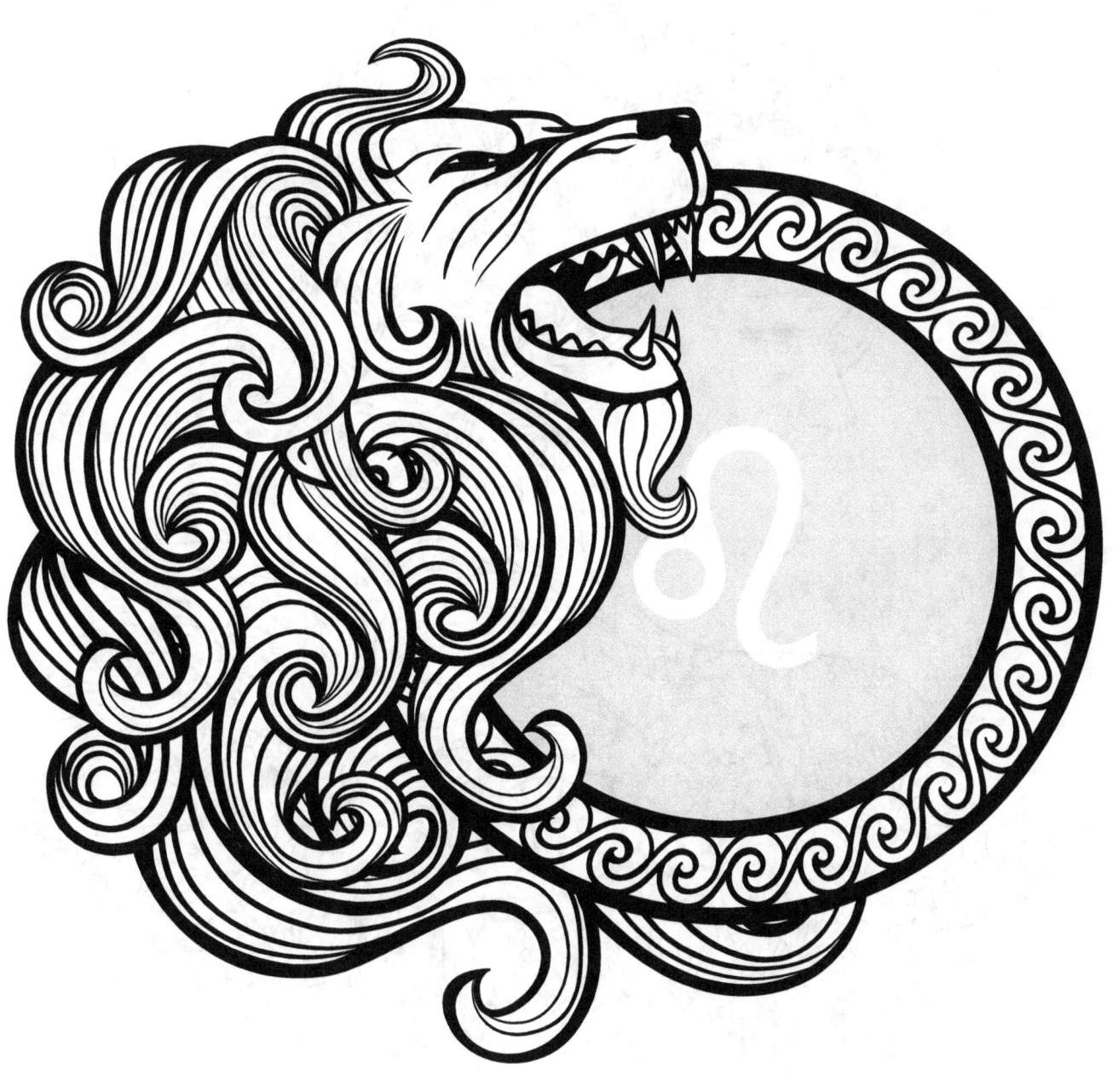

VIRGO

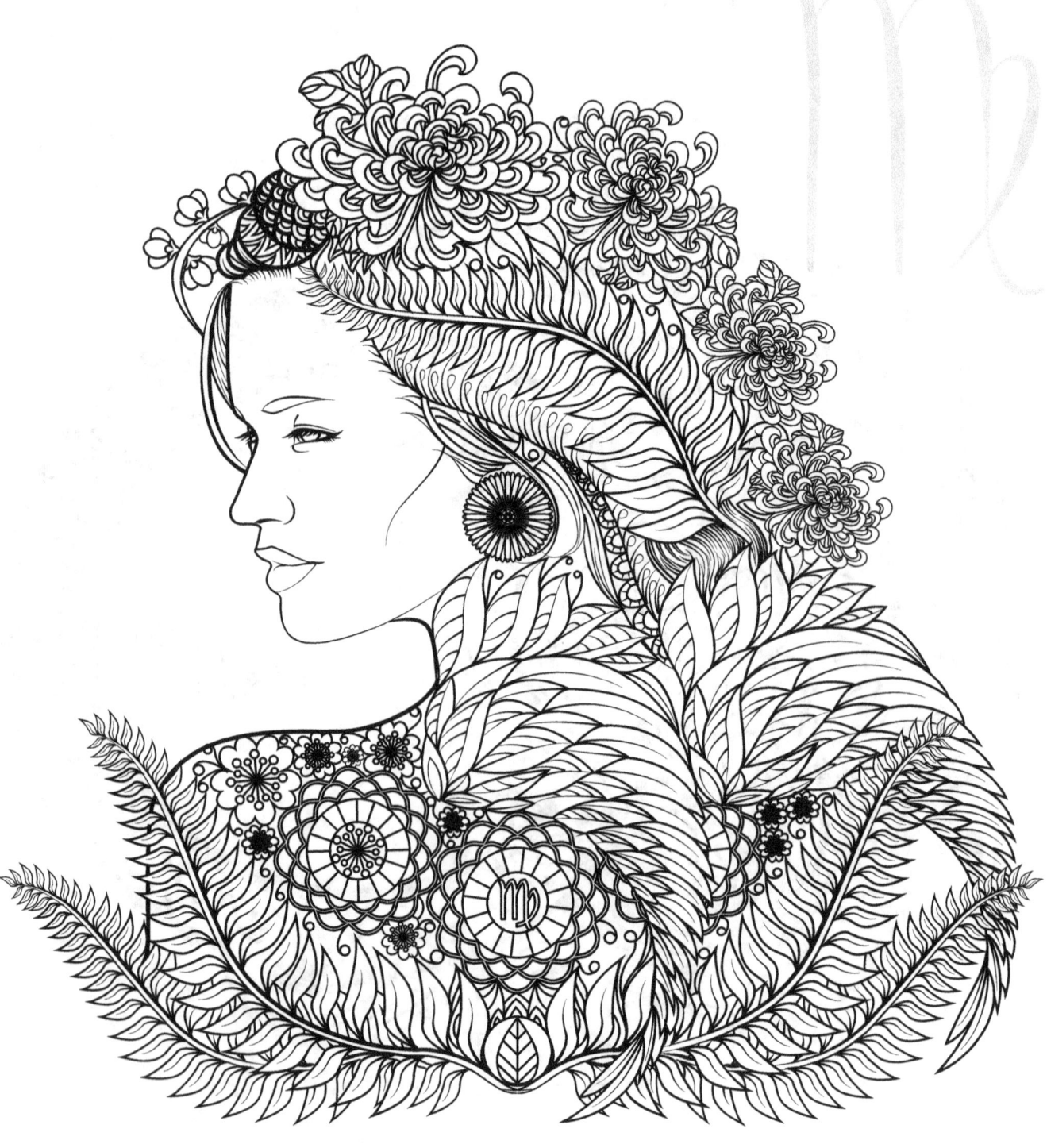

LIBRA

SCORPIO

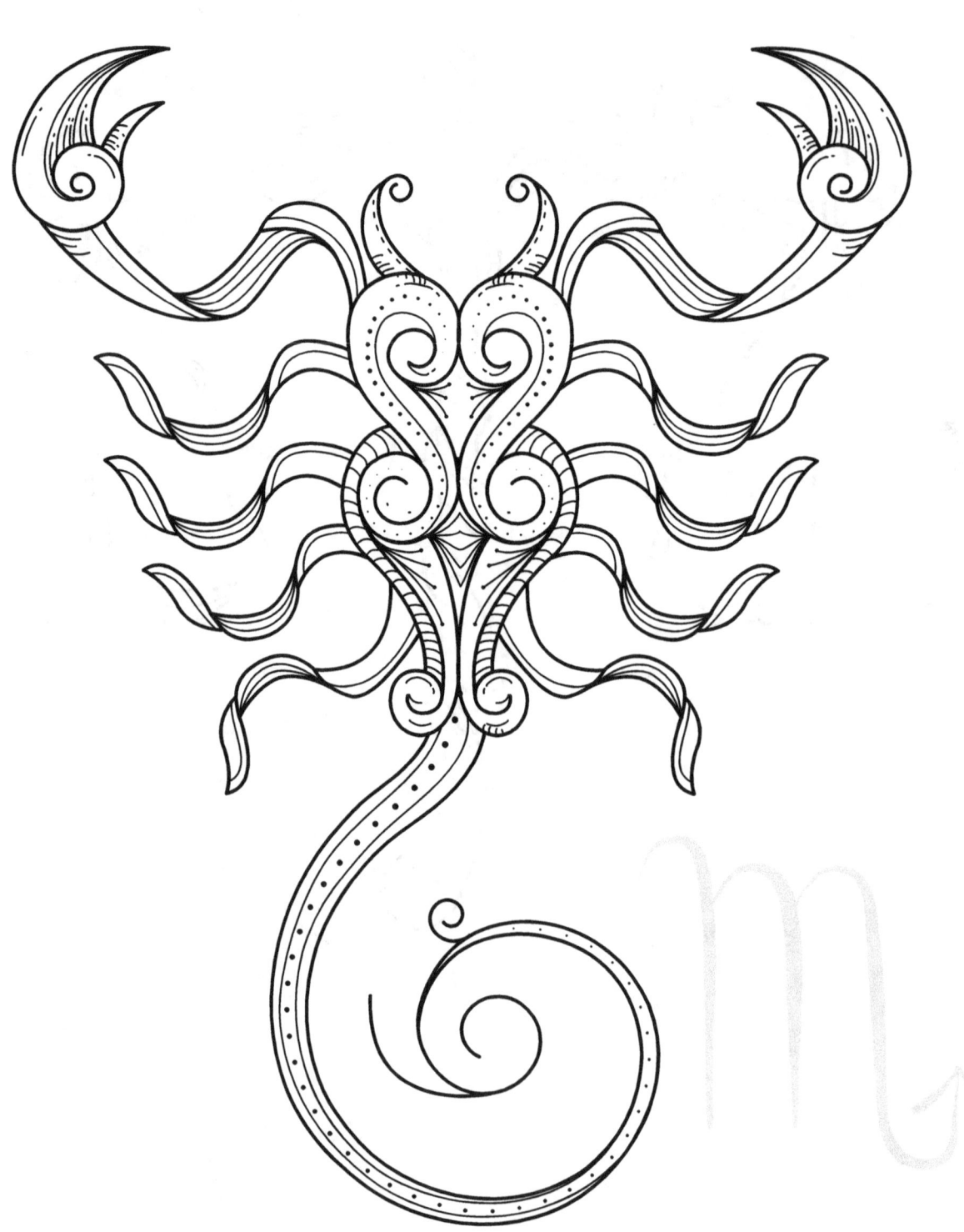

SAGITTARIUS

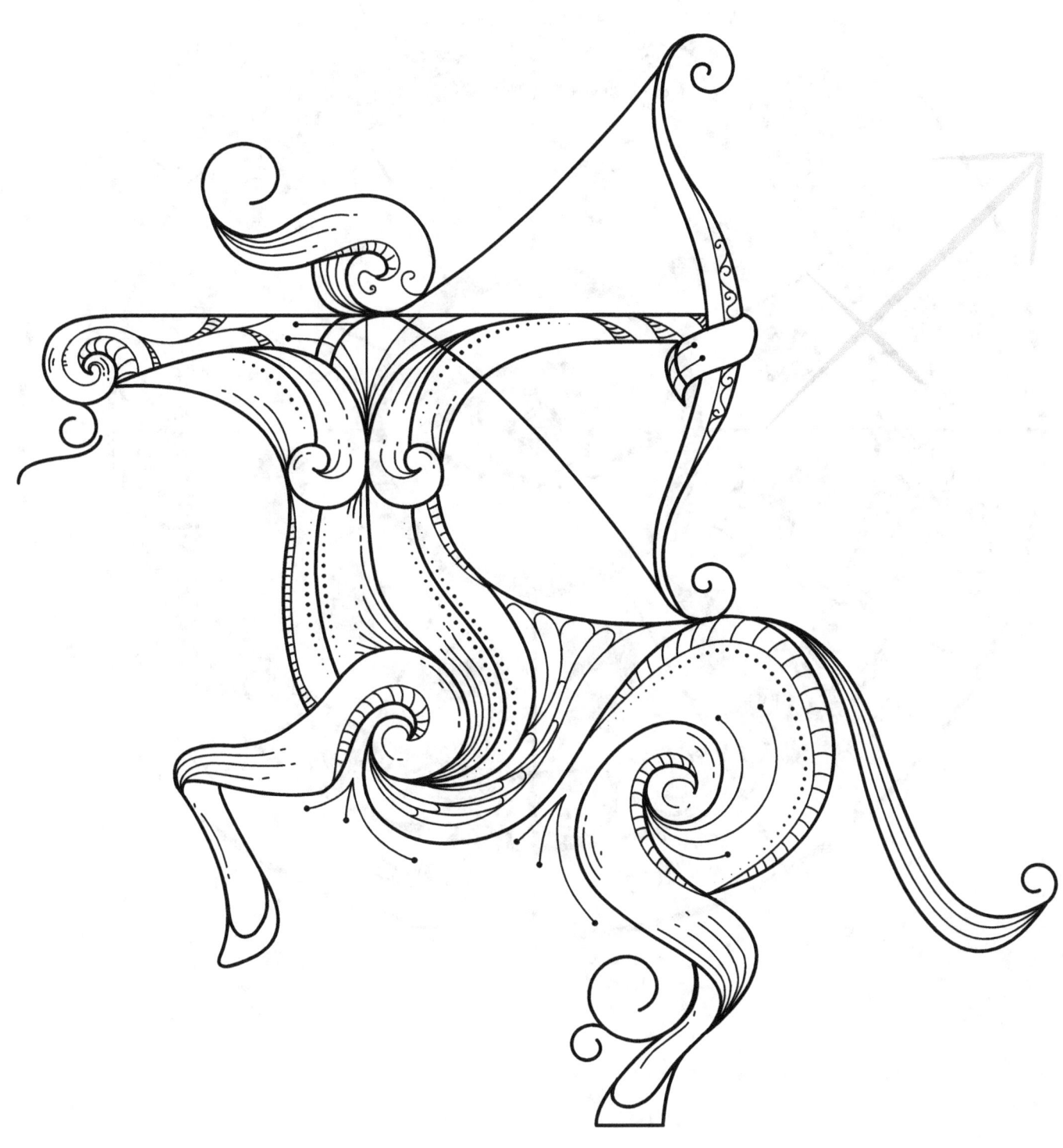

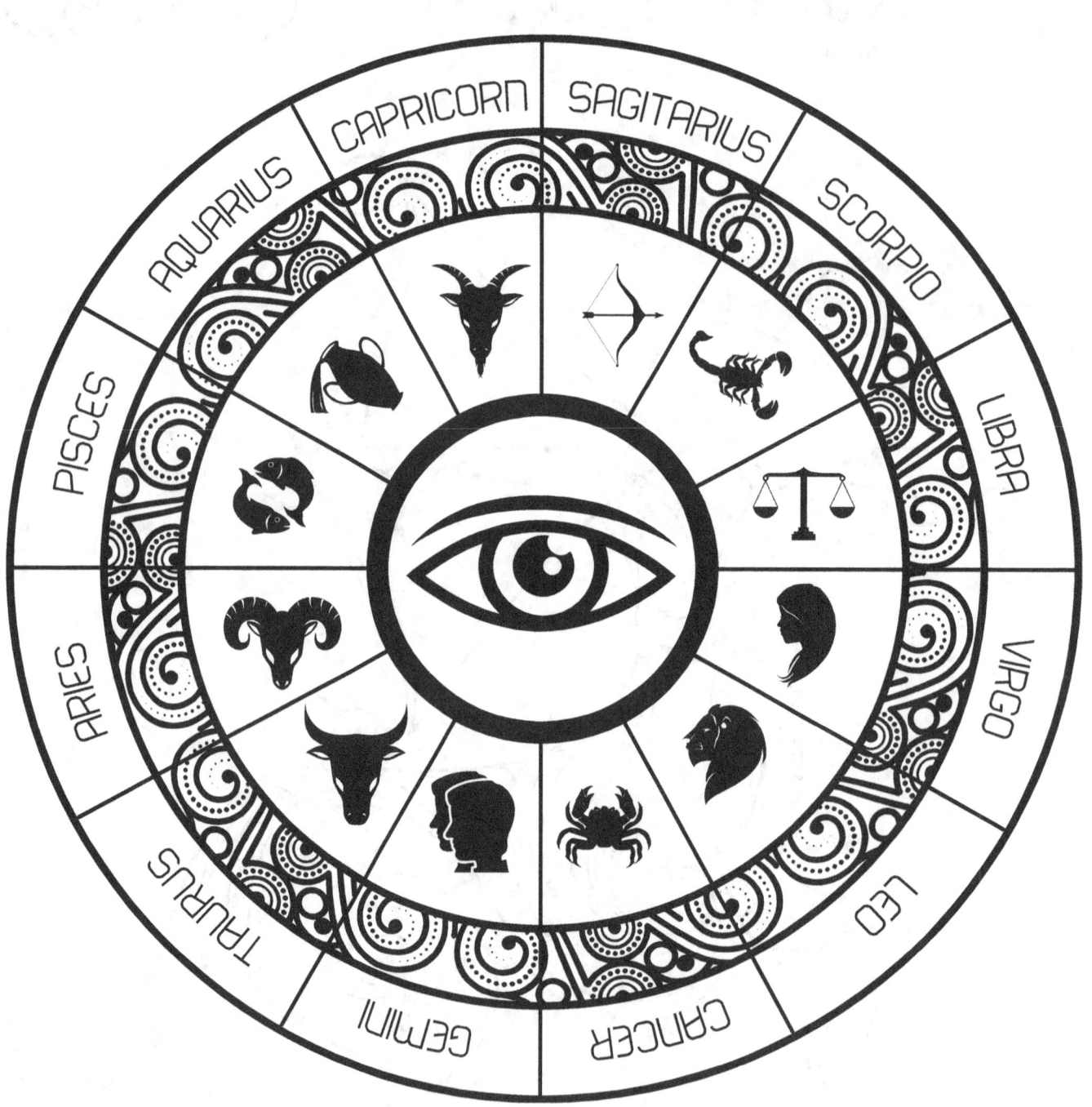

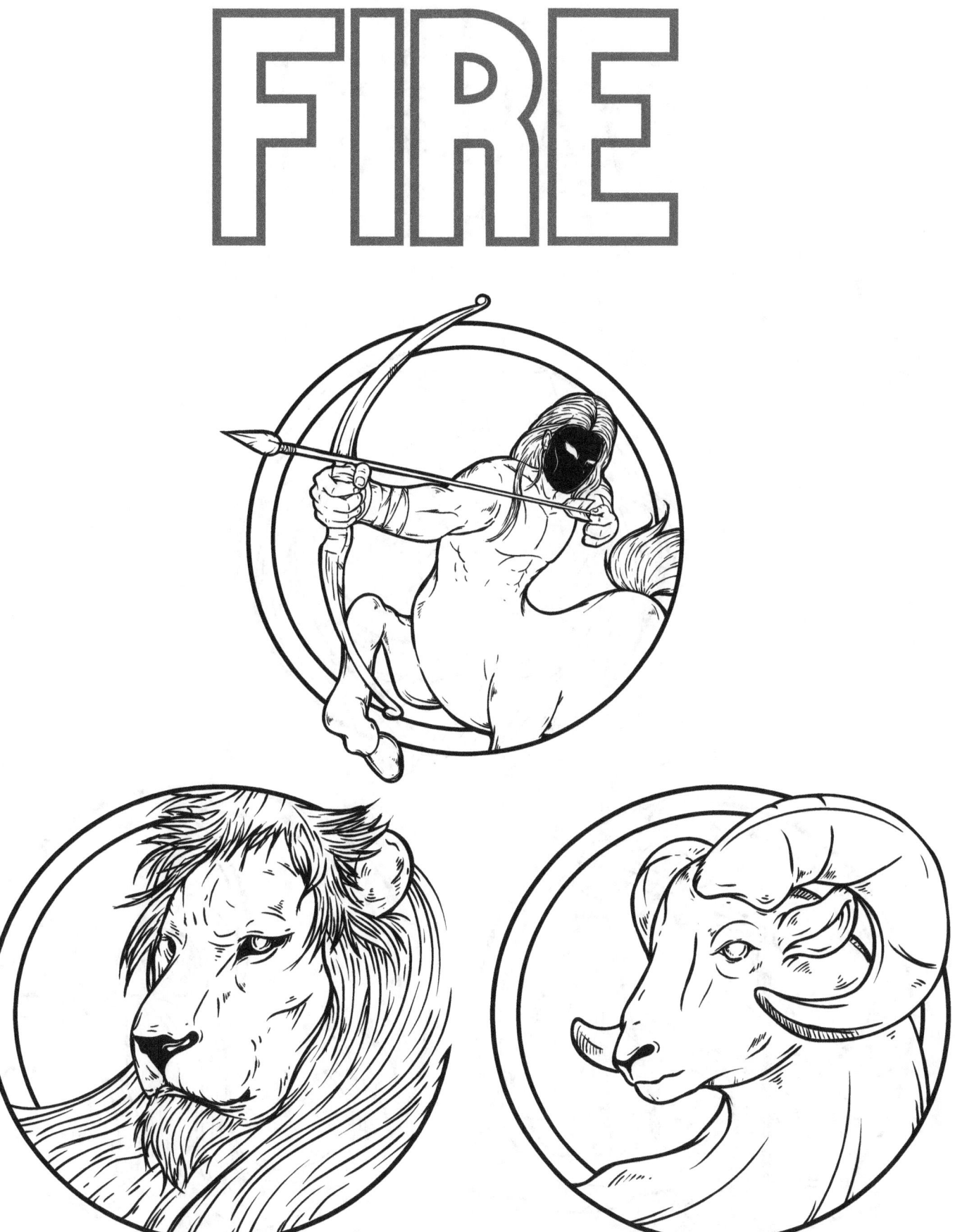

AIR

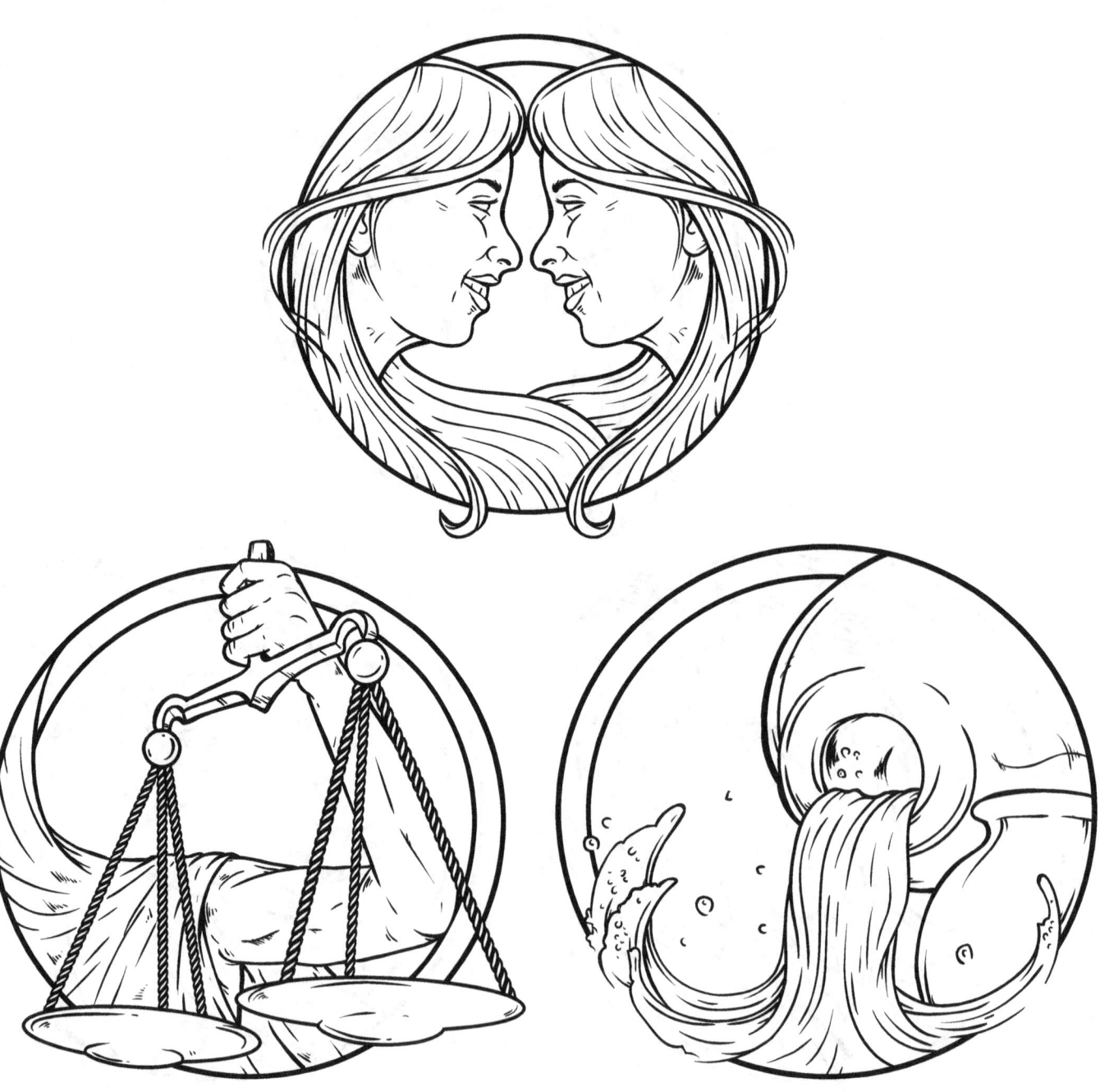

WATER

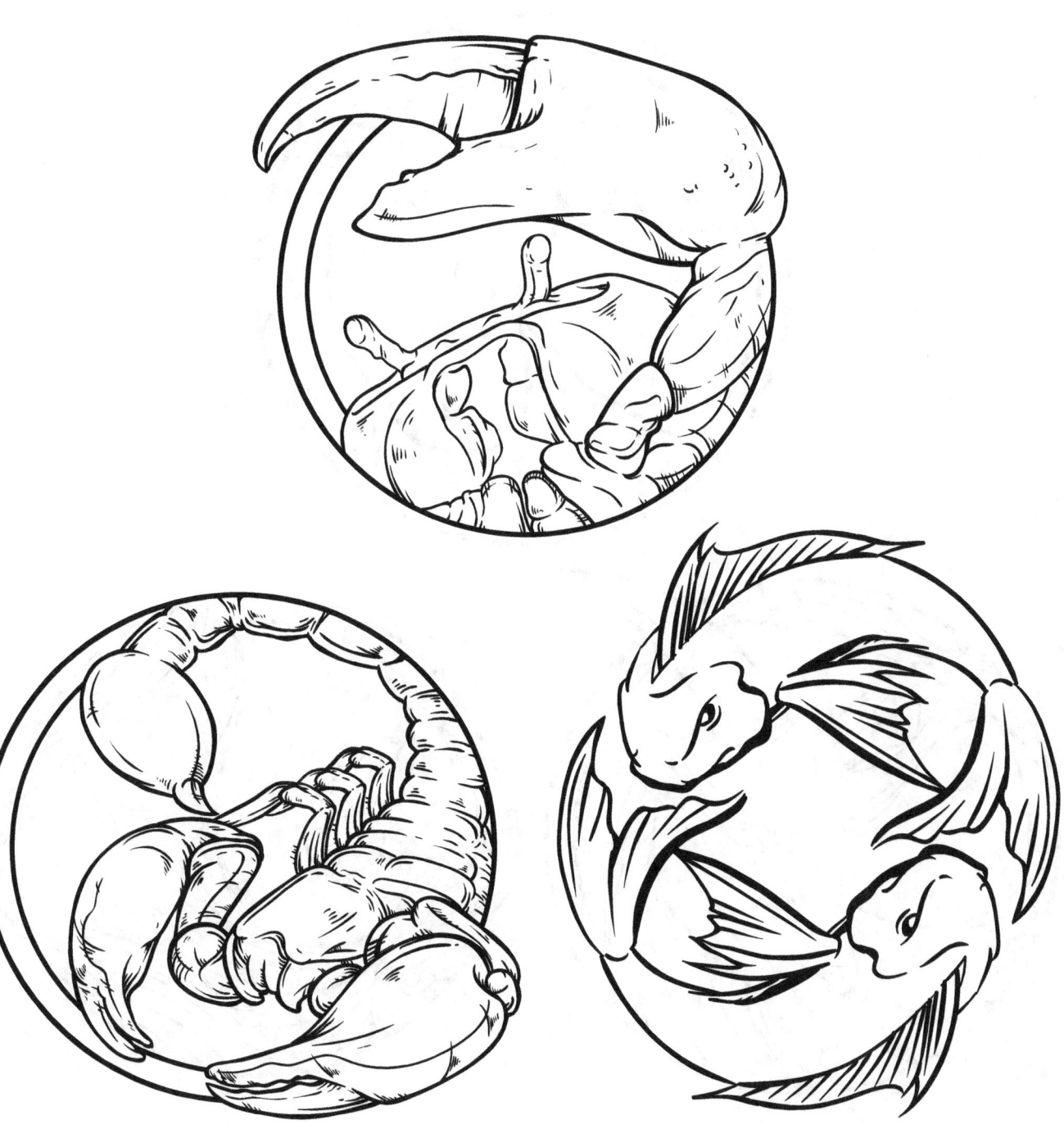

EARTH

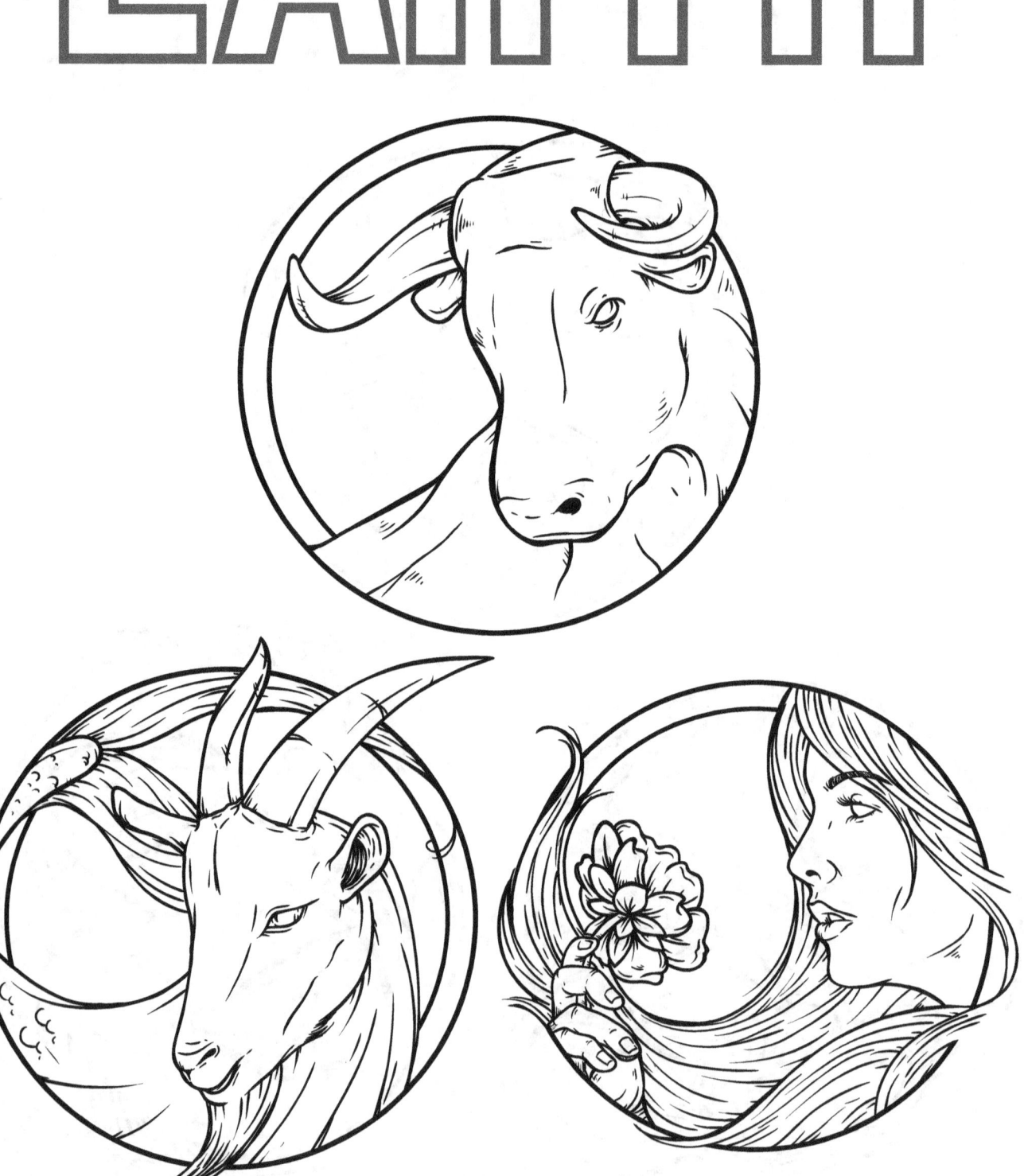

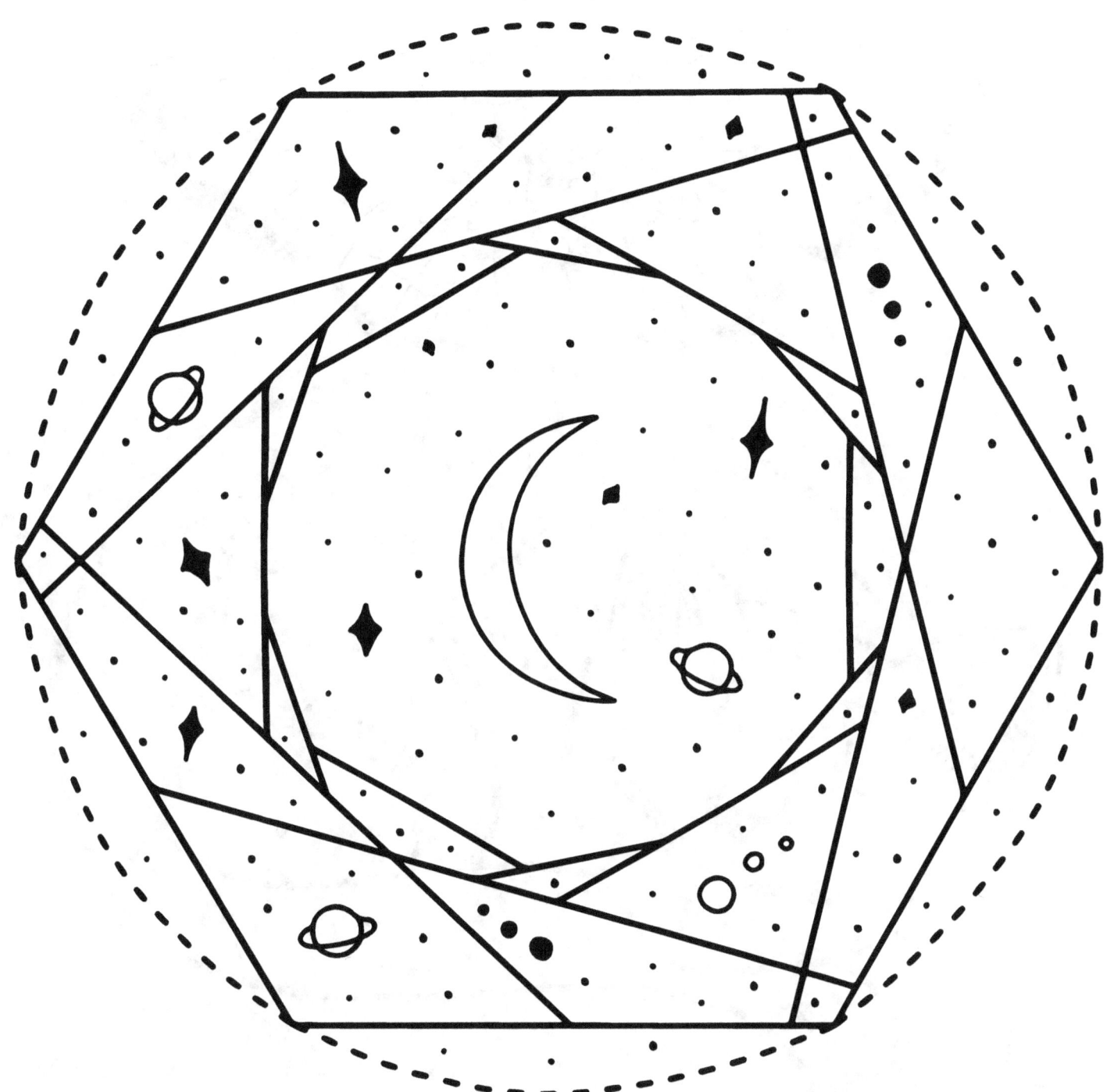

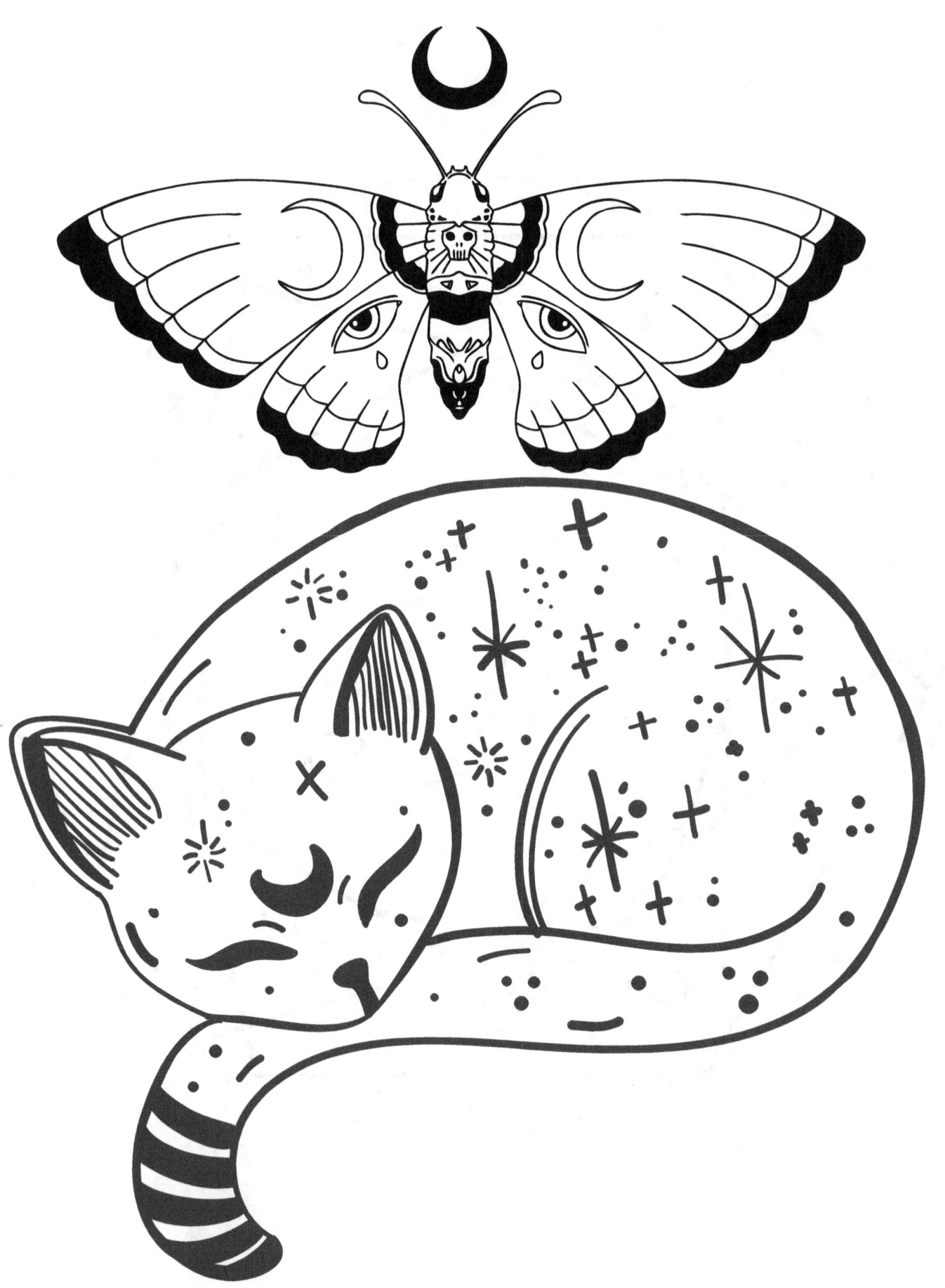

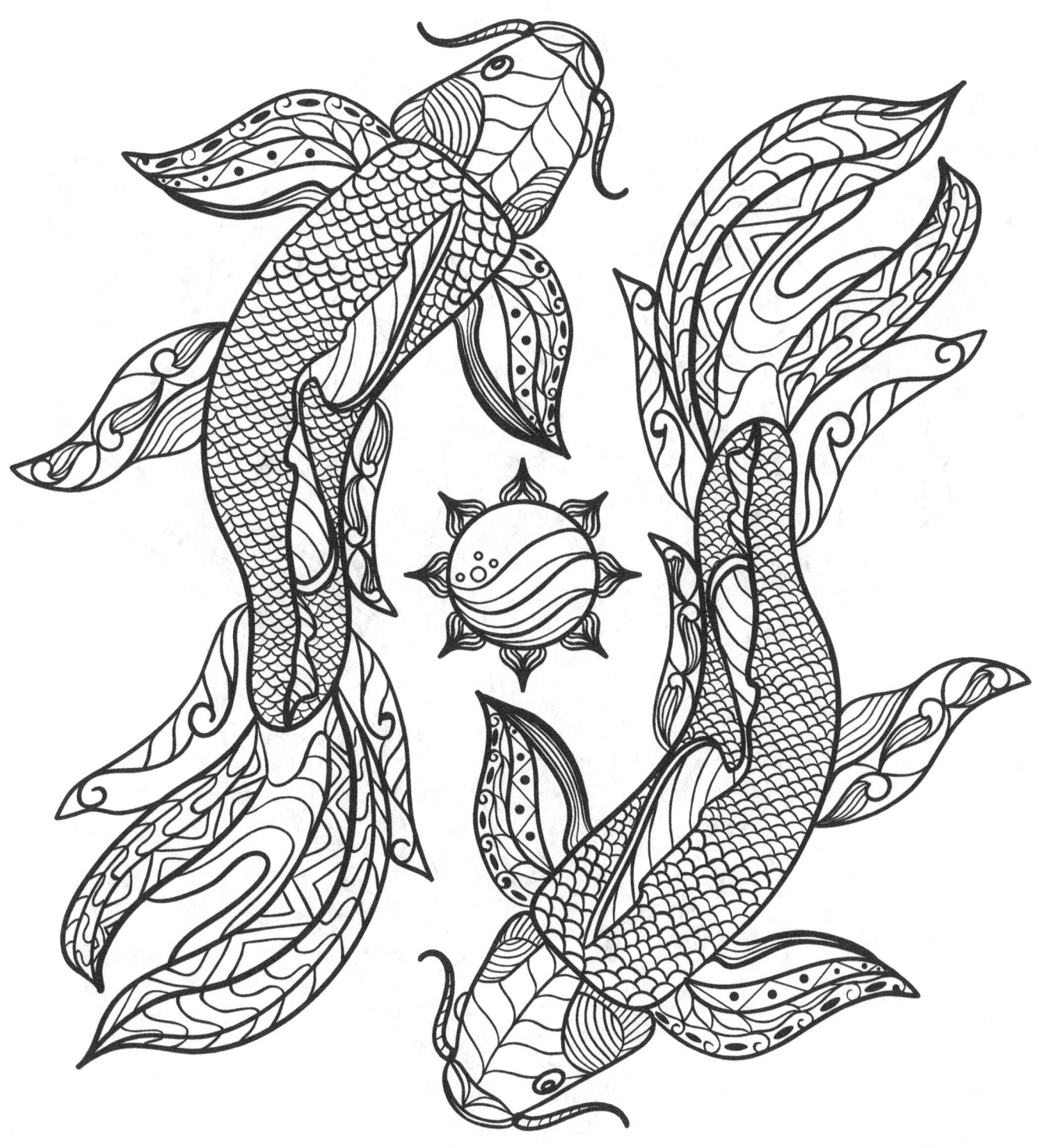

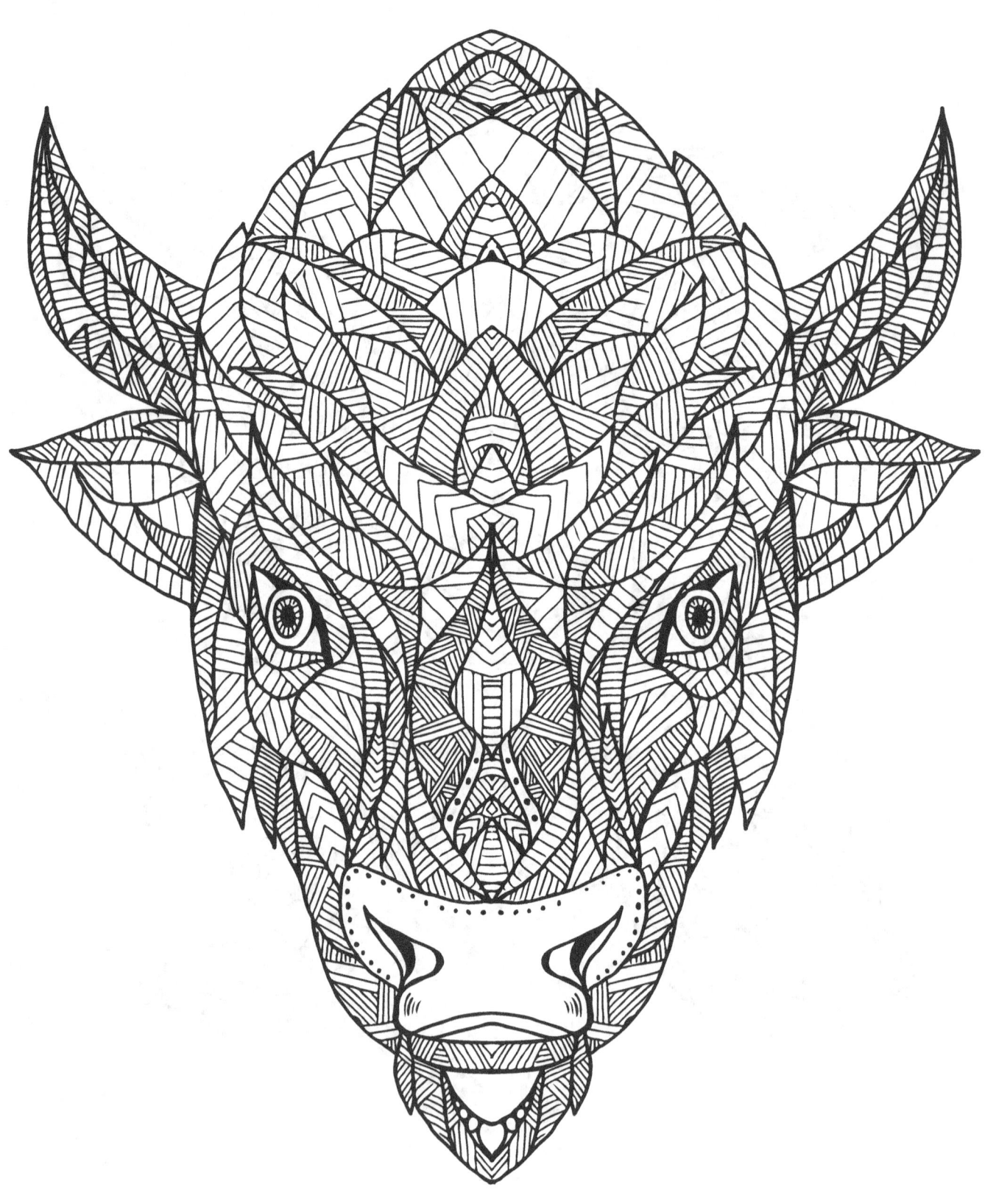

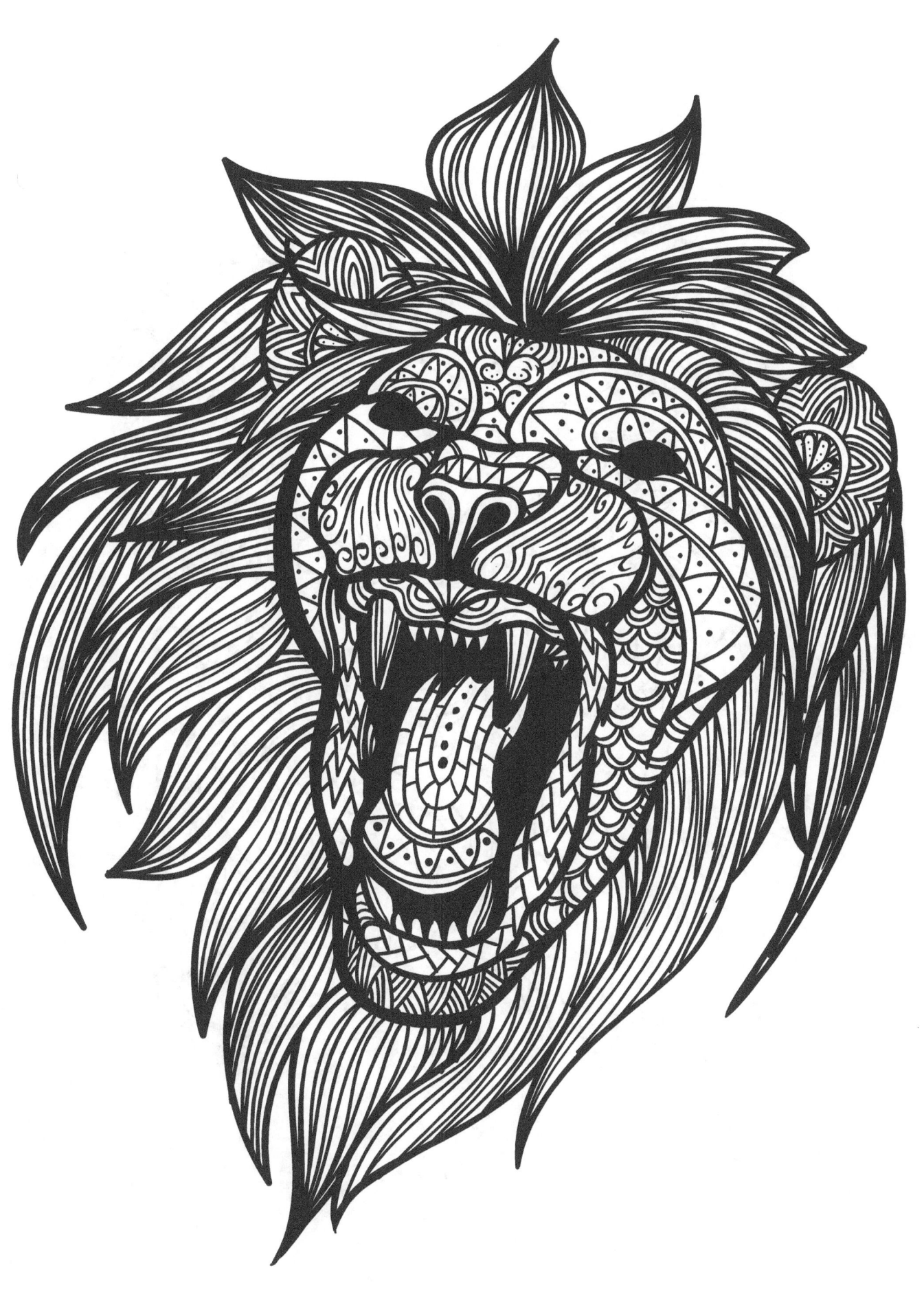

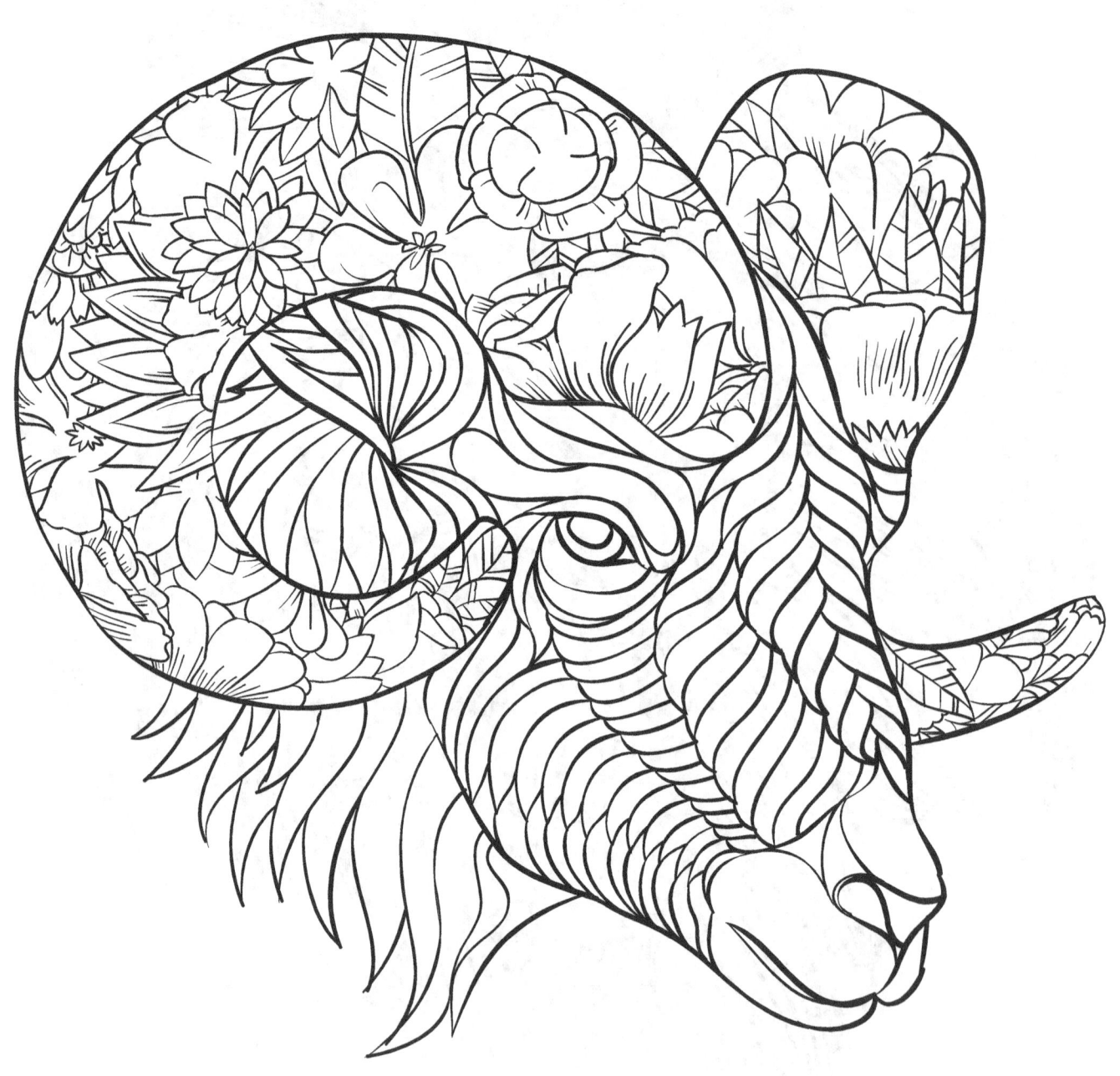

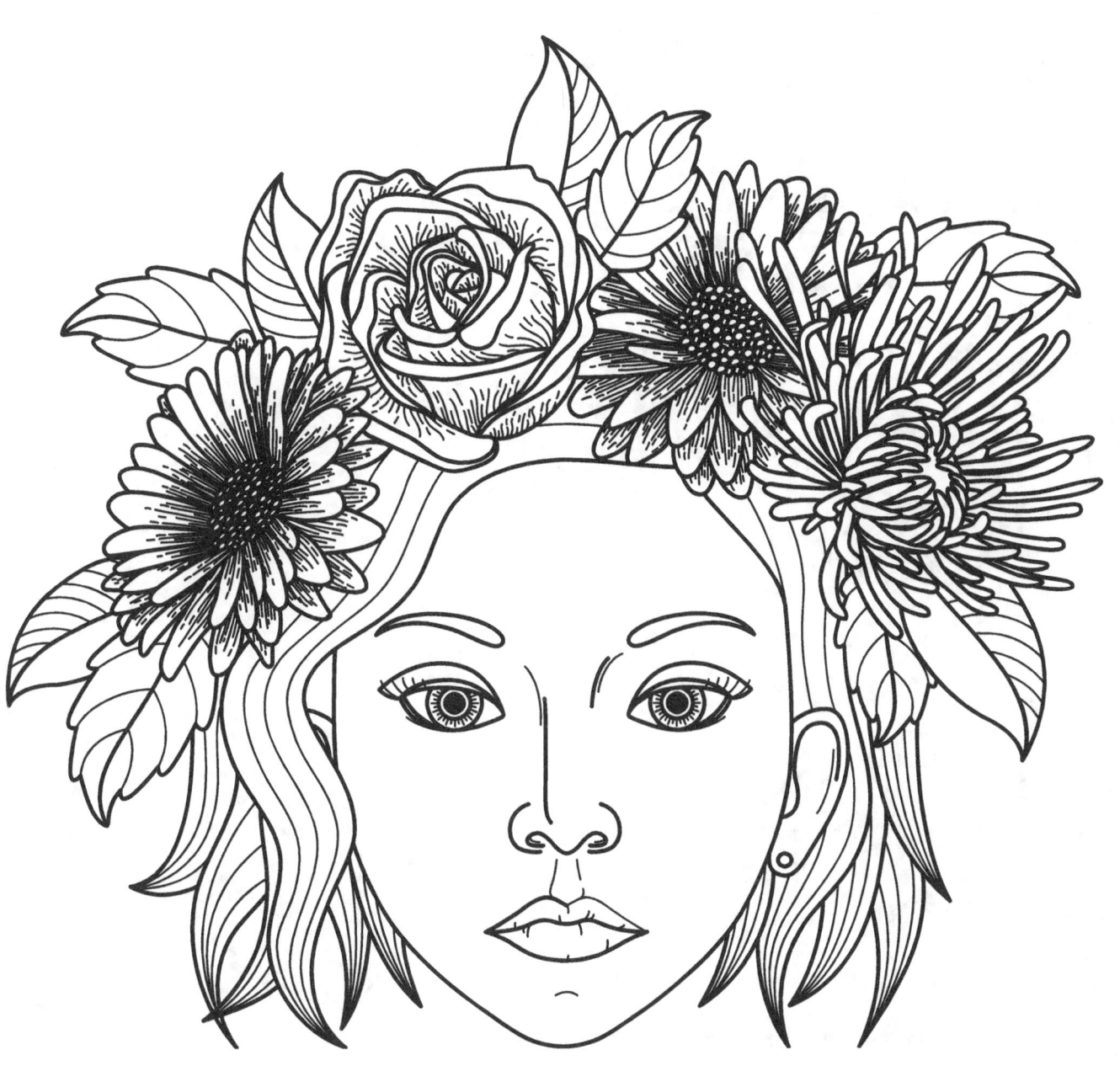

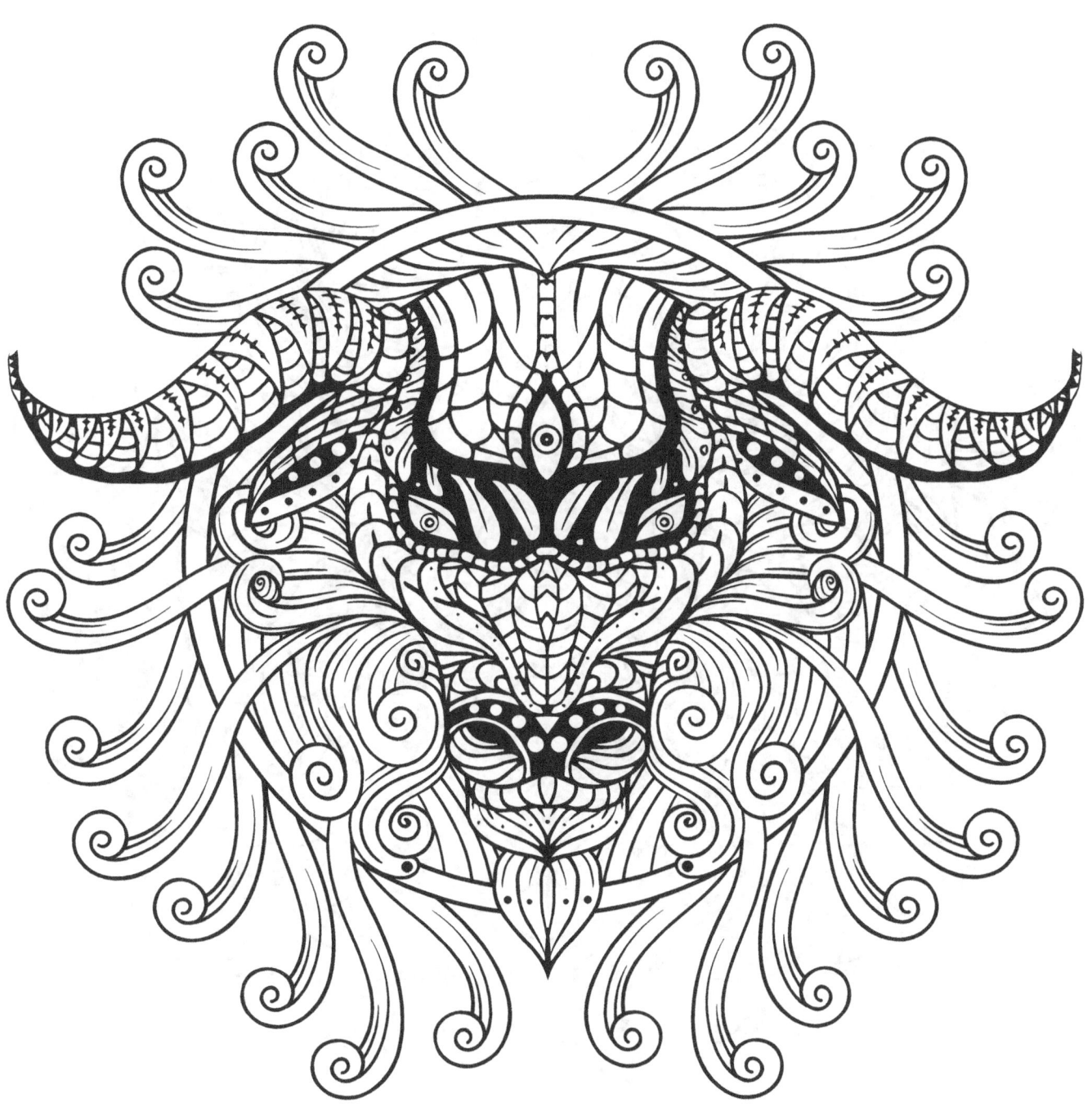

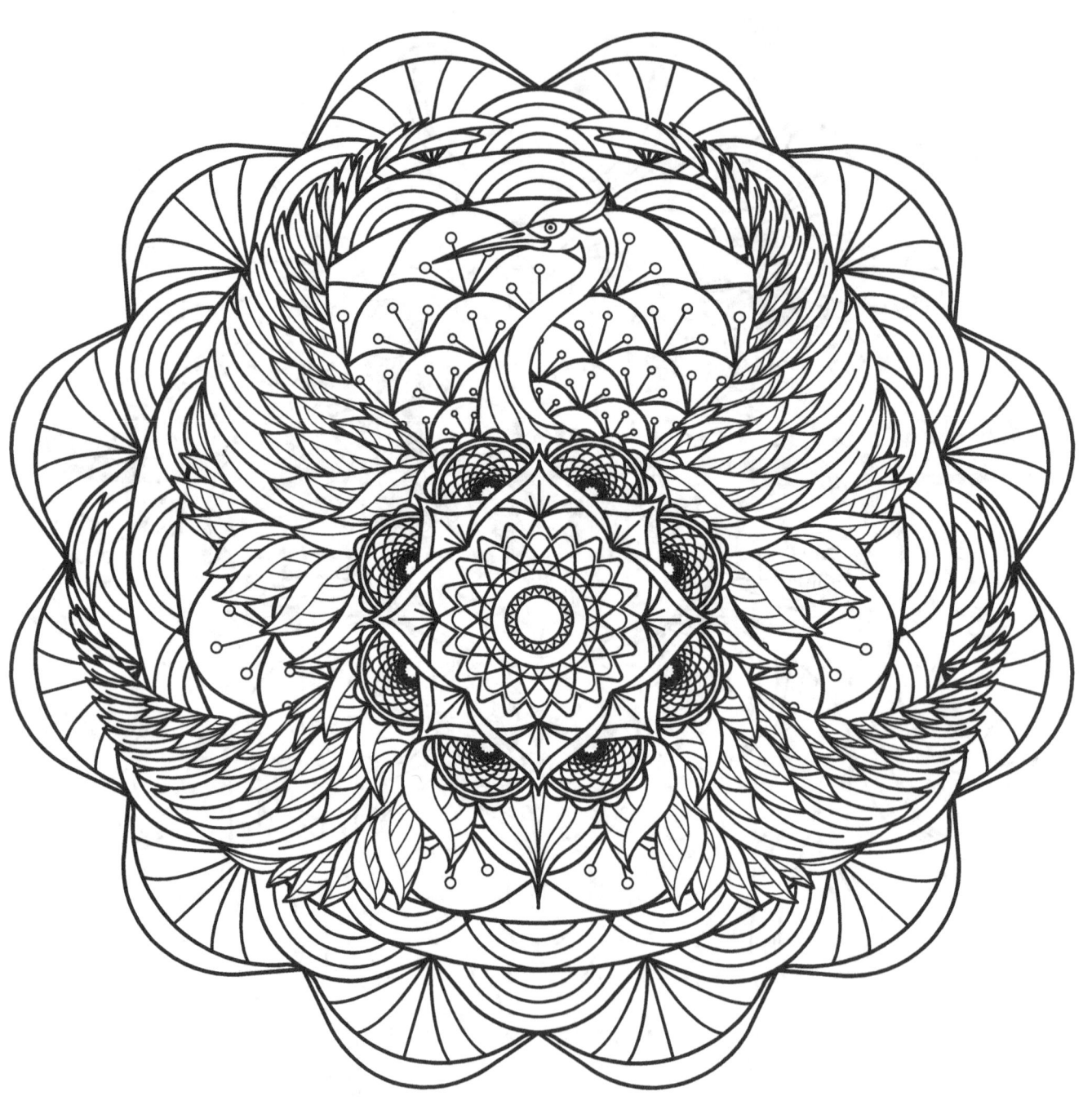

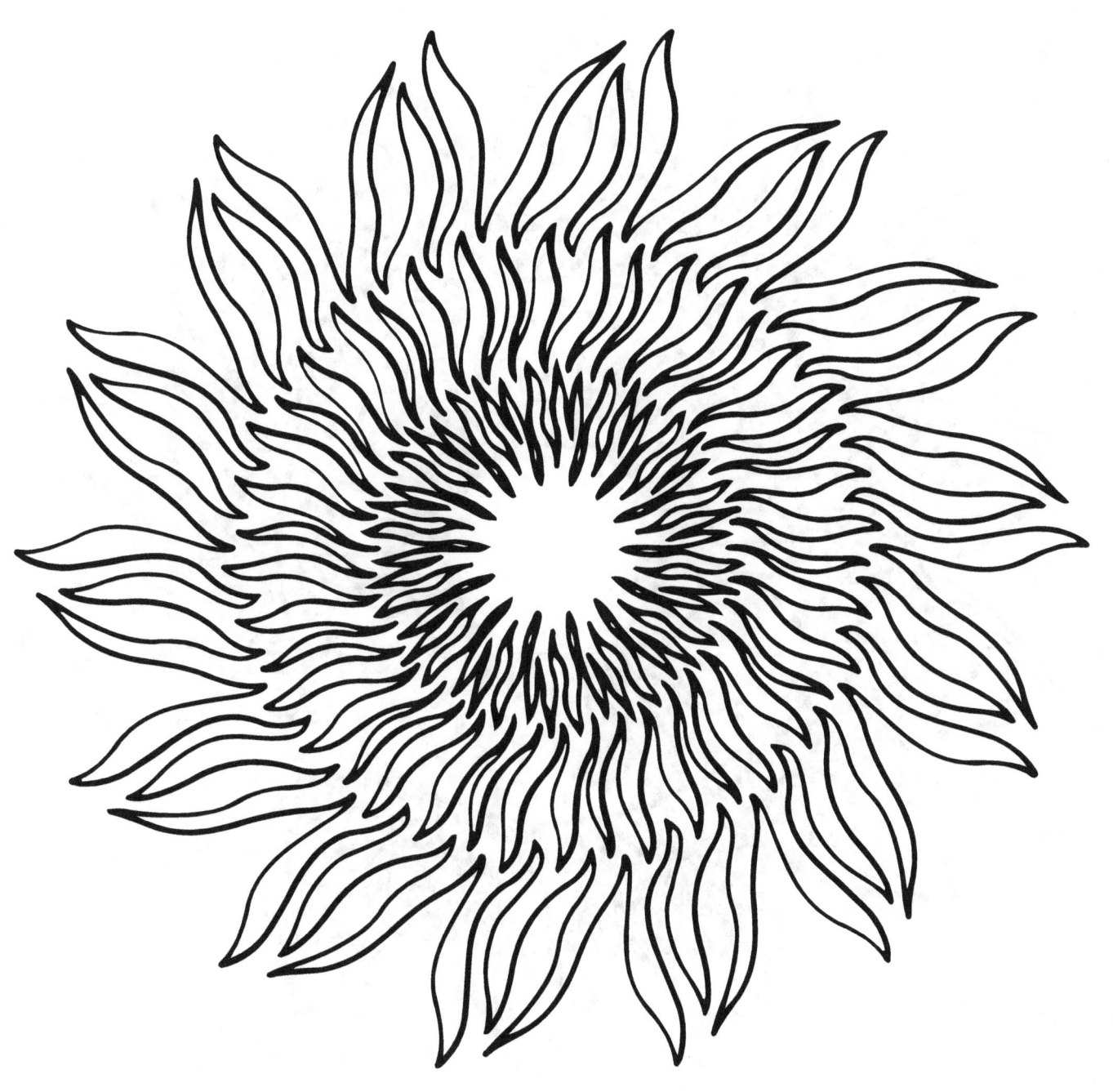

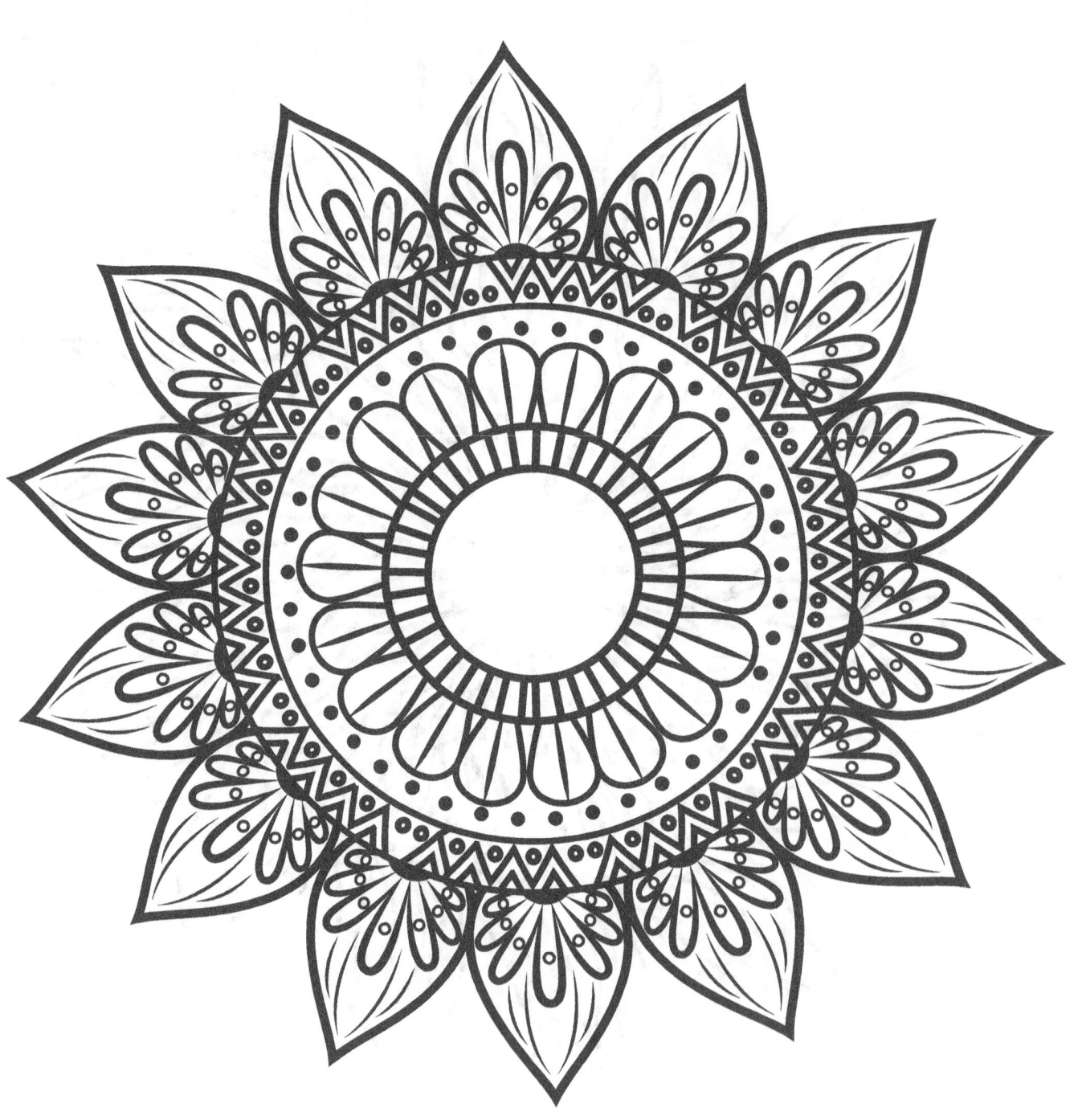

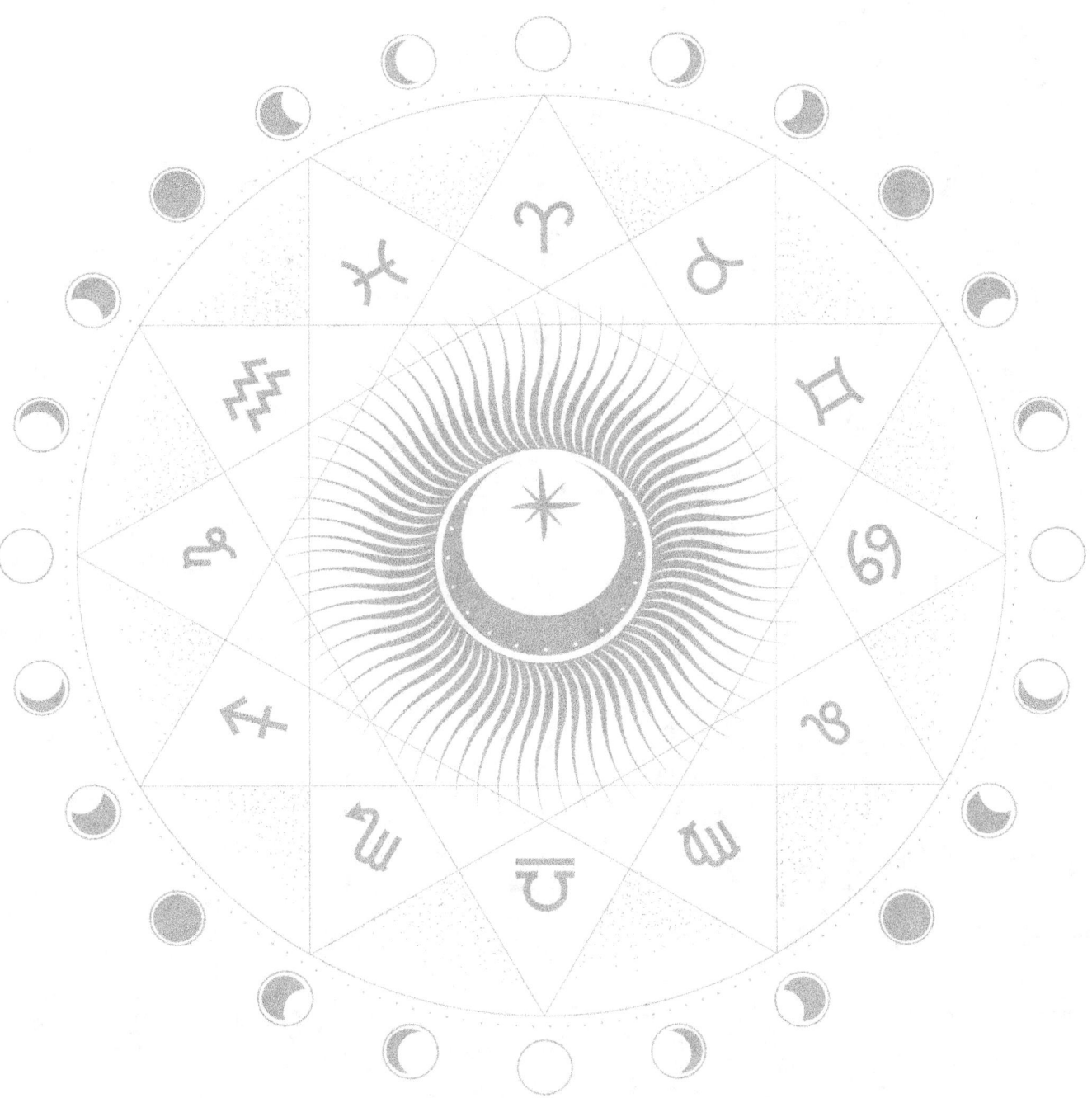

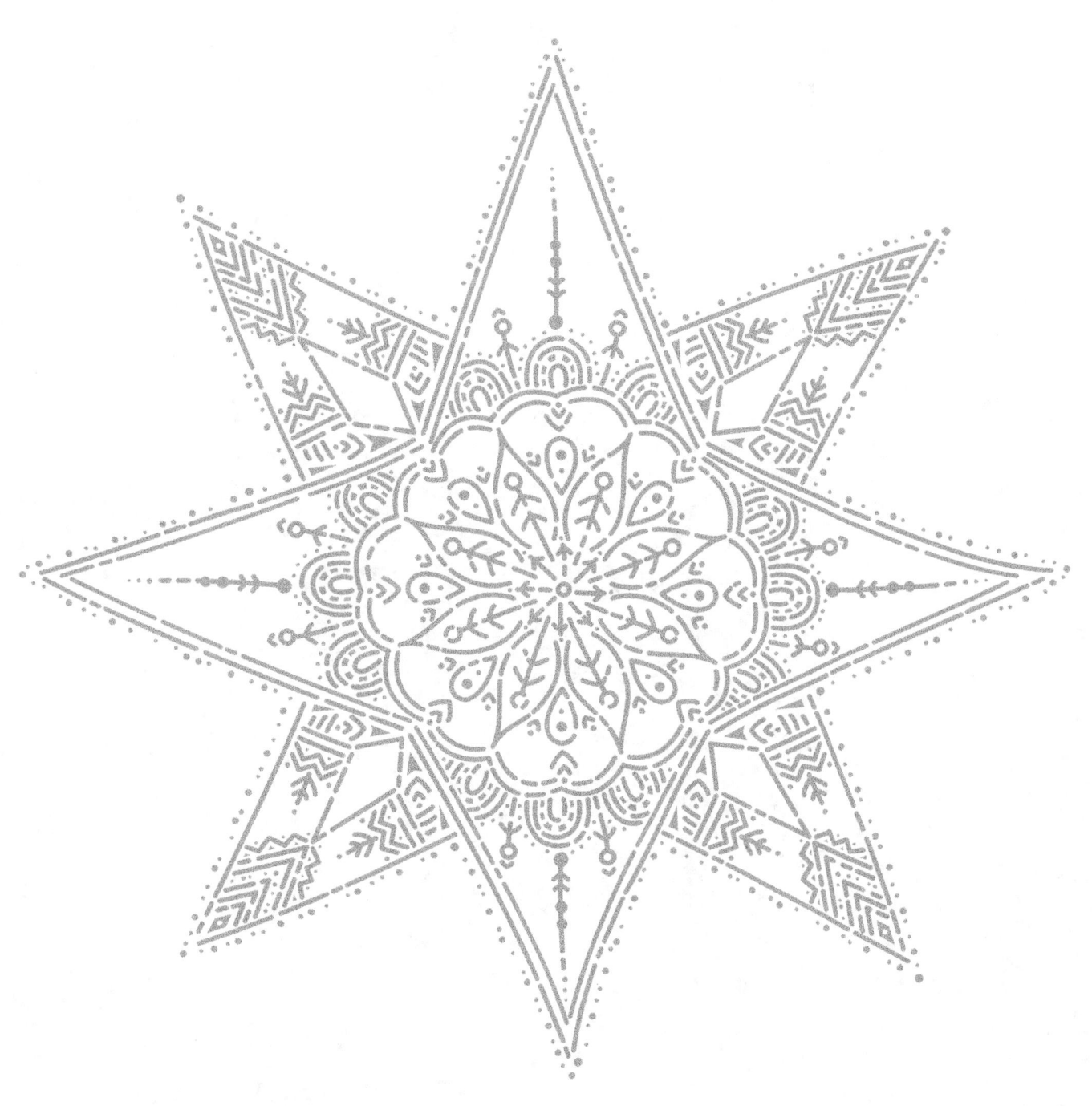

www.ingramcontent.com/pod-product-compliance
Lightning Source LLC
Chambersburg PA
CBHW080439220526
45465CB00009B/3346